# Step by Step

## Learning to Follow Jesus
## (Based on the Principles of *Steps to Christ*)

**Jerry D. Thomas**

*Teaching Tips by*
**Jerry and Kitty Thomas**

**Pacific Press® Publishing Association**

Nampa, Idaho
Oshawa, Ontario, Canada
www.pacificpress.com

Cover design by Gerald Monks

Inside design by Bruce Fenner

Illustration credits:
Cover photos copyright iStockphoto.com and dreamstime.com
Cover picture of Jesus by Darrel Tank
All Interior photos copyright iStockphoto.com

Unless otherwise noted all scriptures quoted are from ICB, the *International Children's Bible, New Century Version,* copyright © 1983, 1986, 1988 by Word Publishing, Dallas, Texas 75039. Used by permission.

Scripture marked NIV are taken from the HOLY BIBLE, NEW INTERNATIONAL VERSION®. Copyright © 1973, 1978, 1984 by International Bible Society. Used by permission of Zondervan Publishing House. All rights reserved.

Scriptures marked NCV are quoted from *The Holy Bible, New Century Version,* copyright 1987, 1988, 1991 by Word Publishing, a division of Thomas Nelson, Inc. Used by permission.

Library of Congress Cataloging-in-Publication Data

Thomas, Jerry D., 1959-
  Step by Step : learning to follow Jesus (based on the principles the principles of Steps to Christ) / Jerry D. Thomas ;  teaching tips by Jerry and Kitty Thomas.
      p. cm.
  ISBN-13: 978-0-8163-2277-0 (pbk.)
  ISBN-10: 0-8163-2277-5 (pbk.)

  1.  Christian life—Seventh-day Adventist authors—Miscellanea—Juvenile literature.
  2.  Seventh-day Adventists—Doctrines—Miscellanea—Juvenile literature.
  3.  White, Ellen Gould Harmon, 1827-1915. Steps to Christ—Juvenile literature. I. Thomas, Jerry D., 1959- II. Thomas, Kitty, 1959- III. Title.

BX6121.T46 2008
248.4'867—dc22

2008010112

Additional copies of this book are available by
calling toll-free 1-800-765-6955 or by visiting www.adventistbookcenter.com.

08 09 10 11 12 • 5 4 3 2 1

# Dedication

To Ethan,

my new reason to write books for kids

# Other books by
# Jerry D. Thomas

*Conversations With Jesus*

The Detective Zack series

The Great Stories for Kids series

*Messiah*

The Shoebox Kids series

The Shoebox Kids Bible Stories series

*What We Believe for Kids*

# Contents

# Introduction

The purpose of this book is to help kids take their first steps in Christian discipleship. It's to help them understand what it means to be a Christian, to understand how a Christian grows and matures. Based on principles drawn from Ellen White's classic book *Steps to Christ*, this book isn't meant to be comprehensive or deep, but simple and understandable for children. Certainly there are other principles that could be emphasized, but these seemed to me to be the most important beliefs for children to grasp.

The Teaching Tips section will assist any teacher, parent, or caregiver who is trying to help children begin their walk with Jesus and help children understand why Christians say and do the things they do. By tying these principles and beliefs into a concrete story or experience, we make them more real and more meaningful. By attaching them to experiences that children can identify with, we make them a part of the children's identity as Christians.

Use the Teaching Tips with individual children, Sabbath School classes, or Bible lessons in the classroom. Adapt them to meet the needs of the children you are reaching.

Every child is different, and each one will have different questions as they seek to understand.

In the back of the book is a selection of quotations from *Steps to Christ* that form the basis of the teachings of each chapter. If you're also beginning your walk with Jesus, or struggling to find your way, spend some time considering what those words can say to your heart.

I have written a great deal for children, and in those words I've tried to follow the example of Jesus by using simple stories to convey great truths. When you're trying to teach children great truths, you don't try to tell them everything—you try to tell them the most important things in words they can understand.

Like *What We Believe for Kids*, this book is the brainchild of Aileen Andres Sox, the beloved editor of *Primary Treasure®* and *Our Little Friend®*. Mrs. Sox continues to develop ways to make faith more real to children, and it's been my privilege to assist her.

Jerry D. Thomas

# Learning to Follow Jesus

I think it's fun to follow a path through the woods or across a field. Even if I don't know where the path is going, I like to follow along to see what's over the next hill or behind the next tree! Being a Christian is like following a path that Jesus left for us. And the further we go, the more we learn to be like Him! That's what we're going to talk about in this book—following Jesus so we can be more like Him!

# We Learn That God Loves Us

## Bible Verse

" 'For God so loved the world that he gave his one and only Son.' "

—John 3:16, NIV

Did you see the sun come up this morning? Are you sure that it did? I'm sure it did—it came up and shone right in my eyes while I was trying to sleep! Even when we don't see the sun come up, we know it has because it gets light outside. Even when it's cloudy or stormy, we know that the sun is up there shining. And at night, even though it's really dark, we know that the sun will still come up the next morning.

As we begin to follow the path Jesus left us, there's one thing we need to be sure about. We need to know that God loves us. Just like we're sure that the sun will come up every morning, we can be sure that God loves us. Just like nothing can stop the sun from rising, nothing can stop God's love for us—nothing!

One of the ways God tells us that He loves us is through nature. God knows that we like things that are pretty. So when we see a bright yellow sunflower or a red, red rose, that's one of the ways God is saying, "I love you." He knows we like things that are cute and funny. So when we see a puppy chasing its tail or a kitten pouncing on a leaf, that's another way God is saying, "I love you!" I think God likes to see us laugh—I think that's why He gave us giraffes and kangaroos!

Whenever we're outdoors, we can see that God is caring for the plants and animals by giving them rain to drink and their own special kind of food to eat. When we see mountains or the ocean or rainbows or stars, we know that God is bigger and more powerful than we can imagine. But all the things that we see tell us one thing loud and clear—God loves us!

And knowing that is the first big step on Jesus' path.

## Teaching Tips

1. Discuss with the children the ways we know that our parents or grandparents love us. What do they do or say? How is that similar to what God does for us?

2. Have each child make a list of his or her favorite ways that God shows His love. They may begin with their favorite animals or flowers. Remind them to include personal pets, possessions, or even parents. Don't let them forget about the gift of Jesus.

3. Collect pictures that show how big and powerful God is. Photos of galaxies or planets in space, mountains, storms, or other scenic views might be collected on the Internet and shown in a PowerPoint presentation. If you're worried that the kids won't find them interesting, include photos of cute animals.

### Summary

Just like we're sure that the sun will come up every morning, we can be sure that God loves us.

# We Learn What God Is Like

## Bible Verse

" 'God gave his son so that whoever believes in him may not be lost, but have eternal life.' "

—John 3:16

Do you know what the earth looks like? I know it's round like a ball, and that it has tall mountains and blue oceans and green trees and brown deserts. But when I stand outside my house, I can't see the ocean or any big mountains. I can't tell what the earth looks like by looking at a part of it, because it's too big.

But I do know what the earth looks like, because I have a globe. A globe is a round picture of the earth. Mine is about the same size as a basketball, and it shows where there is ice and where there is desert on our planet. It shows the water and the land. By looking at my globe, I can tell how far it is from my house to the ocean or to the mountains. I can't see the whole earth, but I can learn a lot about what it looks like by looking at my globe.

Last time, we talked about being sure that God loves us. But God is bigger and more powerful and more amazing that we can imagine. How can we know what He is really like? He gave us a way to know Him better—He gave us His Son, Jesus. " 'God loved the world so much that he gave his one and only Son so that whoever believes in him may not be lost, but have eternal life' " (John 3:16).

Like a globe tells us what the earth is like, the story of Jesus tells us what God is like. When we learn that Jesus was always fair and truthful, we know that God cares about doing the right thing. When we learn that Jesus healed sick people and cheered up those who were sad, we know that God cares about how we feel. When we learn that Jesus never hurt another person and was always kind, even to those who hurt Him, we know that God loves every person—including us.

The more we know about God, the more we want to be like Him. And that's the next big step on Jesus' path.

## Teaching Tips

1. Have fun with the children by helping them figure out how far it is from where they are to the closest mountain or the closest beach or to some other significant landmark. Show them on a globe, if possible.

2. Pick several stories of Jesus, such as the healing of the lepers or the feeding of the five thousand, and ask, "What does this story tell us about God?"

3. If you're familiar with working with papier-mâché, help the children make a globe by pasting strips of paper onto a round balloon. After the globe dries, it can be painted to look like the earth. Remind the children that a globe shows us what the earth is like and Jesus shows us what God is like.

### Summary

As a globe tells us what the earth is like, the story of Jesus tells us what God is like.

# We Learn Why God Loves Us

*"The Father has loved us so much! He loved us so much that we are called children of God."*

—1 John 3:1

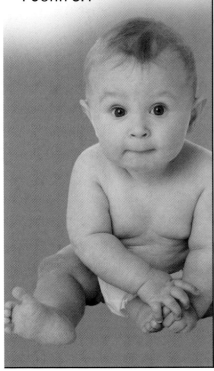

Have you ever seen a brand-new baby? They're not always the cutest things in the world! Sometimes their skin is really red and wrinkled. Sometimes they don't have any hair, or they look like they got a really bad haircut. Usually, they're either sleeping or crying.

But if you've been around a new baby, you know this is true: everybody seems to love them! Everyone thinks they're so sweet or cute or beautiful. Why is that?

I can tell you why. The first time I saw the faces of each one of my children when they were born, I loved them. I knew right then that I would do anything in the world to help them or protect them. Did I love them because they were beautiful? No, they were wrinkly and red. Did I love them because of the things they could do for me? No, all they did was cry and sleep. There's only one reason why I loved them—they were my children.

It's the same way with God. He doesn't love us because we're tall or short. He doesn't love us because we have straight teeth with no cavities or perfectly combed hair. He doesn't love us because we read our Bibles or because we go to church. He doesn't love us because we're nice to others or because we always tell the truth.

He loves us because of who we are—His children. He loves us no matter what we do or say. He doesn't love us more when we're good or less when we get into trouble. He loves us just because we exist, just because we are alive. He loves us because we are His children. And nothing will ever change that.

When we know why God loves us, we know that nothing can ever make Him stop loving us. And knowing that is the next big step on Jesus' path.

## Teaching Tips

1. If possible, show a newborn baby or photos of a newborn to the children. Discuss how the baby has wrinkled skin or no hair or a misshapen head. Review why people love new babies—and why God loves us.

2. Have the children make a list of various descriptions of people: tall or short, young or old, ones who pray or ones who don't pray, ones who live in America or ones who live elsewhere, etc. Divide the list into things that make God love people and things that don't. Make the point that none of these things are on the list of why God loves people.

3. Help the children make posters by pasting a photocopy of one of their baby photos on a sheet of paper. Under their photo, have them write, "Why does God love me? Because I am His child."

### Summary

God loves us just because we exist, just because we are alive. God loves us because we are His children. And nothing will ever change that.

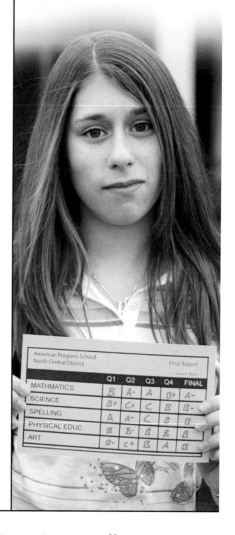

# We Learn What We Can't Do

*"Can a person . . . change the color of his skin? / Can a leopard change his spots?"*

—Jeremiah 13:23, NCV

When I was growing up, I had a friend whose skin was darker than mine. Whenever we played out in the sun in summer, I got sunburned, but she didn't. "I wish my skin were as dark as Jackie's," I said to my mom.

"You can wish all you want," she answered, "but it won't change the color of your skin."

I decided that Mom must be wrong. "I'll spend every day outside until my skin is darker." So every day I played outside. By the end of the summer, I was taller. I could run and climb trees faster. And my skin did get a little darker, but my tan quickly faded back to pale. It's still pale today. Nothing I did changed the color of my skin.

Our next step in following Jesus is to learn what we can't do. Because of sin, all humans are born selfish. If it wasn't for God, we would spend our whole lives angry and mean, caring only about what we want. But God is working on every person's heart—even those who don't believe in Him—trying to teach them that being kind will make them happy.

One of the first steps in following Jesus is learning that no matter how hard we try, we can't make ourselves good without Him. Oh, we can grit our teeth and do something nice even when we don't really feel like it, but that doesn't make us good. That doesn't show what's really in our hearts. We can't change our own hearts. Only God can do that.

The Bible says, "Can a person . . . change the color of his skin? / Can a leopard change his spots?" (Jeremiah 13:23, NCV). And the answer is No. Just like we can't change our own hearts. Only God can do that. And knowing that is an important step in learning to follow Jesus.

## Teaching Tips

1. Ask, "Have you ever done something nice or right—like sharing something you have—when you didn't really want to? How did it make you feel? Does it feel different when you want to share?" Point out that sharing brings joy if you want to do it.

2. Find coloring sheets of a variety of animals. Challenge the children to color them differently, to change them. What would an elephant look like with stripes, or a tiger with a lion's mane? What about a zebra with spots or a cat with a curly tail? Remind them that we can't change ourselves. Only God can change us.

### Summary

We can't change our own hearts. Only God can do that.

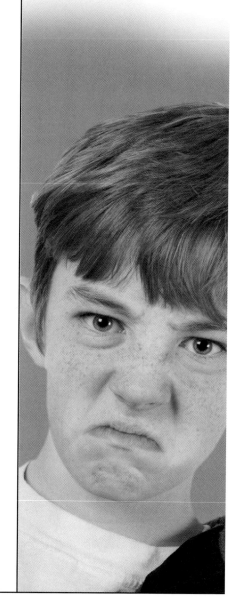

# We Learn That Jesus Connects Us to Heaven

**Bible Verse**

*"Jesus answered, 'I am the way. And I am the truth and the life. The only way to the Father is through me.' "*
—John 14:6

What is the longest ladder you've ever seen? Have you seen the ones that firefighters use? How would you like to climb to the top of a ladder like that? Can you think of other people who use ladders in their jobs? How about painters, carpenters, and decorators?

Now that you've thought of so many people who use ladders, answer this question: why do people use ladders? The answer is simple—they need to reach something they can't get to on their own.

The Bible has a story about a ladder that was taller than any of the ones we've talked about. Jacob was in trouble. He had just tricked his father into making him the next boss of the family instead of his brother Esau. His father was very sad and disappointed, and Esau was mad enough to kill him! So Jacob ran away from home. He left so quickly that he didn't take a tent or sleeping bag or anything. That night he lay down on the ground and used a rock for a pillow. Jacob was tired and lonely, and he felt really bad about what he had done. He was afraid that God was angry with him and wouldn't help him anymore.

But when Jacob fell asleep, he dreamed about a bright golden ladder that stretched all the way from heaven to earth. Angels were going up and down the ladder, and a Voice told Jacob that God was still with him.

Last time we learned that we can't change our own hearts and become good people. Only God can change us, and this is how He does it. The ladder in Jacob's dream was like Jesus. He connects us to heaven. Even when we make mistakes and hurt others, Jesus is there to remind us of God's love. But He does even more for us. When we follow His path, He changes our hearts. The more we learn about Jesus, the more we change. More and more, we start to act like Jesus!

## Teaching Tips

1. Have the children make a list of people who use ladders in their jobs. If there is someone in your church or neighborhood who uses a ladder in this way, ask him or her to visit the class.

2. Ask, "Have you ever tricked someone like Jacob did? Or has someone tricked you? How did you feel?" Emphasize the "fun" of playing tricks versus how bad you feel when someone you tricked is hurt.

3. Help the children draw a ladder with the letters J-e-s-u-s incorporated into the rungs. Talk about how Jesus connects us to heaven.

## Summary

The ladder in Jacob's dream was like Jesus. He connects us to heaven.

# We Learn About Being Sorry When We Do Wrong Things

## Bible Verse

*"God, you will not reject a heart that is broken and sorry for its sin."*

—Psalm 51:17

Here's a story with two different endings: I was walking through our house one summer day holding a football in one hand. I was on my way out to the yard to play. As I passed by my mother in the kitchen, she said, "Don't play with that in the house."

"Yes, Mom," I said without thinking. Then I thought, *I could toss this football up in the air and catch it a hundred times without dropping it—inside the house or outside.* So I tossed it up—and it bounced off my hands into a flower vase that went crashing to the floor. I could hear Mom running in from the kitchen before the football even stopped bouncing. From the look on her face, I knew I was in trouble. *Oh, no,* I thought. *Mom is going to take away my football or make me work to buy a new vase.* So as soon as she came in, I said, "Sorry! Sorry! Sorry! It was an accident!"

The second ending changes the story just a little. I tossed the football up—and it bounced off my hands into a flower vase that went crashing to the floor. I could hear Mom running in from the kitchen before the football even stopped bouncing. From the look on her face, I knew how much she liked that vase. *Oh, no,* I thought. *That was one of Mom's favorite vases. And I broke it by being stupid.* Before she could say anything, I said, "I'm sorry, Mom. I knew better. It's my fault. I'm sorry I broke your vase."

In both endings, I say that I'm sorry. But which one shows that I'm really sorry for breaking the vase?

There's a difference between being sorry that we're in trouble and being sorry that we hurt someone. People who are following Jesus sometimes do the wrong things. But when we think about what we've done, it makes us sad that we hurt someone else, and we never want to do that again. That's what it means to really be sorry. When we're really sorry and we don't want to do that anymore, we're taking another big step on Jesus' path.

## Teaching Tips

1. Ask, "What's the difference between something you do accidently and something you do on purpose? Can you be sorry for something you did on purpose?"

2. Create a list of events in which children do something wrong, such as taking something that isn't theirs, kicking a football that hits a cat, saying something mean, etc. Include both things done on purpose and things done accidently. Ask the children what they might say in each situation if they were sorry for being in trouble or if they were sorry for hurting someone else.

3. If you have a class or group of children, work with them to act out a play re-creating a variation of the story above in which children do something wrong and then say they are sorry. Acting out the story may help them grasp what it means to really be sorry.

### Summary

There is a difference between being sorry that we're in trouble and being sorry that we hurt someone.

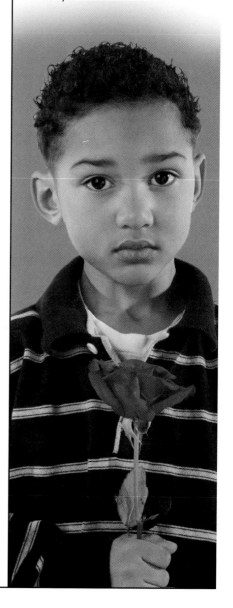

# We Learn That Really Being Sorry Means Changing

**Bible Verse**

*" 'If my people . . . will pray and seek me and stop their evil ways, . . . I will forgive their sin.' "*

—2 Chronicles 7:14, NCV

Do you like to play volleyball? It's fun, but it's not easy to hit the ball right. If you hit it too hard, the ball goes out of bounds. If you don't hit it hard enough, it doesn't go over the net. If you're like me, sometimes when you hit the ball, it goes sideways and hits another player in the head!

One thing I like about volleyball is that each player has a space where they play. When the ball comes into your space, you're supposed to hit it. One day I was playing volleyball with a lot of people from church. I waited and waited, then the ball started coming right to me! I got all ready to hit it—but a tall girl stepped out of her space and hit the ball before it got to me! "Oh, I'm sorry," she said. "I didn't see you."

The next time the ball came to me, she did it again. "Oh, I'm sorry," she said. "I was afraid you couldn't get that one." Then she did it again. "Sorry—I thought that was coming to me." Before long, I didn't even bother trying to hit the ball.

No matter how many times she said "Sorry," I didn't believe that she was. Do you know why? Because she just kept stepping into my space over and over. If a person is really sorry for something they did, they stop doing it.

And that's true for Christians too. Jesus is always ready to forgive us when we're really sorry for doing something wrong. He'll keep forgiving us when we make the same mistakes more than once. But if we're really sorry, we really want to stop doing the wrong thing.

When we really want to change the way we act and to live more like Jesus, He promises to help us. The more we learn about how Jesus treated other people, the more we will want to be just like Him.

With every step we take as we follow Jesus, we are learning to be more like Him.

## Teaching Tips

1. Ask, "Jesus will keep forgiving us if we keep making the same mistakes, but what does He really want to do?" Discuss how He wants to do more than forgive us. He wants to change us

2. Write out "When we're really sorry, we want to stop doing it" on small poster papers. Have each child color and decorate their poster, then have the child take the poster home to hang on the wall.

3. If the time is right and you have space for it, try a little volleyball with the children using a balloon for the ball and a string for a net. They'll have fun and work out a lot of energy!

### Summary

Jesus is always ready to forgive us when we're really sorry for doing something wrong. He'll keep forgiving us when we make the same mistakes more than once. But if we're really sorry, we really want to stop doing the wrong thing.

# We Learn to Apologize to People

### Bible Verse

*"Confess your sins to each other and pray for each other. Do this so that God can heal you."*

—James 5:16

One day when I was about ten years old, I was watching an old Bugs Bunny cartoon with my family. I was sitting in one of our metal chairs in front of the couch, and my sister was sitting on the floor next to me. I liked to lean back with my chair on just the two back legs. "Be careful," my mom said. I wasn't worried. I leaned way back, then whenever something funny happened, I'd lean all the way forward and crash the front legs onto the floor. It was a funny show, and I crashed down over and over.

But one time when I leaned forward and hit the floor hard, I felt the chair hit something. My sister had moved over just far enough to get her foot under my chair. When I came down, I crashed right onto one of her toes!

She started crying and grabbed her bare foot. Blood was dripping, and I was scared. Mom put my sister up on the couch and got a towel to stop the bleeding. I kept thinking, *Will she have to go to the hospital? If her toe is broken, will she have to wear a cast all summer?* I had to go lie down on my bed because I started to feel sick.

I wanted to make it better, but I couldn't. I couldn't take away the hurt or fix it if it was broken. There was only one thing I could do. I went back and stood by the couch. "I'm sorry," I told my sister. "I didn't mean to hurt you."

"I know you didn't," she said. Before long, Mom said that the toe wasn't broken. She put a bandage on the cut, and my sister got to lie on the couch all day. And I was happy to get her a drink or a Popsicle whenever she wanted one!

When we hurt people or do something wrong to them, the Bible says that we should confess or apologize. We should tell them that we're sorry. Then we should tell God that we're sorry. Anytime we hurt another person, it hurts God too.

Sometimes we can fix or pay for something if we break it. Sometimes we can work to make something right again. And sometimes, all we can do is say that we're sorry. But that's an important thing to always remember to do. Because doing that is the next step in learning to follow Jesus.

## Teaching Tips

1. Share a story of your own about hurting someone and having to apologize. Accepting that we will always make mistakes and have to confess or apologize is an important lesson for children to learn.

2. Although the concept of confession as we define it theologically is beyond most children's ability to understand, most of them have some experience with apologizing when they have hurt someone. Introduce the concept of restitution by using the idea of "making it right." Develop a list of situations in which a child does wrong and ask the children how they could make it right. This might include paying for a broken item, returning something taken, or working to pay off damages.

### Summary

When we hurt people or do something wrong to them, we should tell them that we're sorry. Then we should tell God that we're sorry.

# We Learn That God Wants Us to Be Happy

**Bible Verse**

*"God is working in you to help you want to do what pleases him. Then he gives you the power to do it."*

—Philippians 2:13

Bridget was a good dog. She liked to run and chase sticks or balls or anything I would throw. When I put on her leash and took her for a walk, she always pulled me along, hurrying to sniff the next tree or trying to chase a bird. But what she really wanted to do was chase cars! Once she pulled so hard that the leash slipped through my fingers. She raced out into the street, barking and barking as she ran after a car. "Bridget! Bridget, come back!" I shouted as I ran after her.

When I finally caught up with her, she was very happy. She was having a great time! But I was very unhappy. I knew something that Bridget couldn't understand. I knew that if she kept chasing cars in the street, sooner or later a car would hit her and hurt her.

Even though I wanted her to be happy, I wouldn't let her chase cars. Chasing cars might make her happy for a while, but when she got hit by a car, it would make her and me very unhappy. So I kept her inside the yard with the gate closed. Whenever I took her for a walk, I held on to the leash with both hands.

Sometimes we act the same way that Bridget did. We rush to do things that we think might be fun—things like making fun of someone else or sneaking something that doesn't belong to us. But God knows that even if those things are fun for a while, in the end they will make us unhappy. So the Bible tells us not to do those things.

When God tells us not to do things, it's because He wants us to be happy. We may not always understand, like Bridget didn't understand about chasing cars. But if we trust Him, He'll keep us safe so we can have real fun—fun that doesn't hurt us or anyone else.

That's an important thing to remember. And it's the next step in learning to follow Jesus.

## Teaching Tips

1. Take time for some pet sharing. If it's possible, do a show-and-tell and have kids bring their pets. If not, let them tell what kind of pets they have and the things the pets do that get them in trouble. Discuss how we try to keep the pets safe, even if it means not letting them do something they think is fun.

2. Have each child draw something they might like to do that would end up making them unhappy. Some suggestions: going down a big hill very fast on a bike, running through traffic to cross a street instead of crossing at the crosswalk, getting the answers to a test before taking the test, etc.

3. Ask, "What things do your parents tell you not to do because they're protecting you? What things does God tell you not to do because He wants to protect you?"

### Summary

When God tells us not to do things, it's because He wants us to be happy. If we trust Him, He'll keep us safe so we can have fun that doesn't hurt us or anyone else.

# We Learn About Choosing to Believe

### Bible Verse

*"Faith means being sure of the things we hope for and knowing that something is real even if we do not see it."*

—Hebrews 11:1, NCV

Do you remember the time your first tooth fell out? I do. The first thing I noticed was that when I pushed it with my tongue, it moved. It had never done that before! I thought I had done something wrong and broken my tooth, so I decided not to tell anyone. I thought it would get better. But it just got looser and more wiggly. And even though it hurt a little to move it, my tongue kept pushing at it. Then one morning when I was trying to brush my teeth very carefully, my tooth just fell out right into the sink.

I showed it to my mom, and she wasn't unhappy. She smiled and said, "When you lose your baby teeth, that means you're growing up. Put the tooth under your pillow tonight, and the tooth fairy will come and leave you a special gift." I didn't know about the tooth fairy, but I liked the idea of getting a gift, so I put the tooth under my pillow before I went to sleep. And when I woke up, my tooth was gone, but there was a dollar under my pillow! Before long, my brother told me that the tooth fairy wasn't real. It was just my mom who came and left the money. But it was a fun game to play for a while.

We know that the tooth fairy isn't real because no one ever sees it and because we know where the money comes from. But we don't ever see God, so how do we know that He is real? I say we do see God—we see Him each day in the love of our parents, our grandparents, our teachers, and our friends. We learn about Him in the Bible. We believe that rock is hard because we can feel it. We believe that ice is cold because we can feel it. We believe in God because we can feel the difference He makes in our hearts.

We choose to believe in God and to believe that the Bible can teach us to be happy and to be good to each other. And when we choose to believe, we allow God to start changing us into someone who is more like Jesus.

## Teaching Tips

1. Ask, "How do we know these things are real: the sun *(we see it, we feel its warmth)*, the wind *(we feel it, we see it move things)*, your mother's love *(she tells us, she shows us)*, God's love *(we feel it in our hearts, we see it in how others treat us)*?" You'll think of many other examples.

2. Discuss this question: besides the tooth fairy, what other things do people have fun pretending to believe in? Santa Claus and the Easter bunny are two examples. You may think of others. If the season is right, research traditions of Christmas or Easter in other cultures and share them with the children.

3. Assign the children to interview members of the church or their families, or invite the pastor or other guests in, and ask the question, "Why do you believe in God?" Afterward, ask the children for their answers to that question.

### Summary

We believe in God because we see Him each day in the love of our parents, our grandparents, our teachers, and our friends. We believe in God because we can feel the difference He makes in our hearts.

# We Learn That God Wants Us to Have Peace

" 'I leave you peace; my peace I give you. . . . So don't let your hearts be troubled or afraid.' "

—John 14:27, NCV

Do you know what it means when your parents ask for some "peace and quiet"? We all know what "quiet" means: no chasing your sister, no loud TV programs, no practicing on your drums. But "peace" means something else. One of the most peaceful times I remember happened at the end of a long, fun day at my grandparents' house. We had been playing ball in the yard by the lake for hours. Everyone else went inside for a drink of water. I went down to the lake and sat on the boat dock, hanging my feet over the water.

The wind wasn't blowing, and the water was so still it looked like glass. The longer I sat there, the more things I saw. A frog climbed up onto a lily pad by my foot. A turtle floated up to the top of the water only a few feet away. It was so quiet that I heard the wings of the big blue dragonfly that flew slowly past my face.

I remember that I felt good at that moment. I didn't have any homework to do that night. I wasn't in trouble for anything. No one was mad at me. I felt happy and peaceful. I saw a fish swimming past my feet, and I leaned forward just a little bit to see more.

That's when I lost my balance and fell—*splat!*—right in the water. The frog leaped away, the turtle ducked under the water, and the dragonfly buzzed away. The water wasn't deep there, so I stood up and walked a few steps closer to the shore until I could hop back up onto the dock. Then I squished my way up to the house to change clothes.

Jesus wants us to feel peaceful all the time. He said, "I give you peace so you don't need to be worried or afraid" (see John 14:27). As we learn to follow Jesus, we won't do things that make others angry or that make us feel bad. When there are problems, we can trust Him to help us find the answers. And when bad things happen, we'll know that He's with us.

When we feel His peace in our hearts, we know that we're taking another step on the path that Jesus left for us.

## Teaching Tips

1. Ask, "How do you act when you are feeling peaceful? At the dinner table, on the playground, at your desk at school, at night in your bed, or at church? How do you act in those places when you are worried or upset?"

2. Have the children draw pictures that include things that worry them: homework, wars, someone being angry with them, etc. Then have them write across the page, "When I'm worried, Jesus is with me."

3. If it's practical, try playing the quiet game outdoors. Have everyone keep as quiet as possible and listen. What things do they hear? Talk about how things are different when we are peaceful.

### Summary

Jesus wants us to feel peaceful all the time. When there are problems, we can trust Him to help us find the answers. And when bad things happen, we'll know that He's with us.

# We Learn We Can Believe Jesus' Promises

**Bible Verse**

*"No matter how many promises God has made, they are 'Yes' in Christ."*

—2 Corinthians 1:20, NIV

The Bible tells a story of a man who was paralyzed—he couldn't move his arms or legs. Of course, he was sad that he couldn't move. But he was even sadder that it was his own fault. He had lived like every day was a party, eating and drinking things that were bad for him and doing things there were dangerous. He was sad and very sorry for the things he had done. He went to see the priests. They said, "Too bad. This is your fault and God won't forgive you." He went home even sadder.

His friends said, "Let's go see Jesus. Let's hear Him talk and ask Him to heal you." So they picked up his bed and carried him to the house where Jesus was talking. The crowd was so big that they couldn't get their friend to the door. So they climbed up on the roof and cut a hole in it. Imagine how surprised everyone inside was to see the sick man coming down from the sky!

Jesus wasn't surprised. He looked at the sick man and said, "You are forgiven." Right that minute, the sick man felt better. He didn't try to move his arms and legs. He just lay there and smiled. Jesus said that he was forgiven, and he believed it.

But other people didn't believe it, and they didn't like Jesus saying that. So Jesus said, "Just so you know that I do have the power to forgive this man, I'll show you that I have the power to heal him also. Stand up," Jesus said to the man, "pick up your bed and go home." And the man jumped right up and obeyed.

When we do things that hurt ourselves or things that hurt other people, we feel bad about it, just like the sick man did. We feel bad because we are sorry, and when we're sorry, Jesus promises to forgive us. We don't have to wonder if what we did was too bad or if God might be angry with us. Jesus promised to forgive us, and He does.

Believing that is the next big step on our journey with Jesus.

## Teaching Tips

1. For children who have made major, hurtful errors in their short lives, this concept is difficult. Try asking them, "Think about the last time you were in trouble for something that was really your fault. How did you feel? What made you feel better?" Discuss the power of forgiveness.

2. Ask the children to retell the story or act out a drama imagining that it was their house where Jesus was talking and someone cut a hole in their roof. Or what if the story took place at their church and someone cut a hole in the roof while the pastor was preaching?

3. Have fun with this story by acquiring or creating a portable cot that the children could use in a reenactment of the story, taking turns being the sick man and the friends who carry him. Don't let them cut a hole in the ceiling!

### Summary

When we're sorry for having done things that hurt ourselves or hurt other people, Jesus promises to forgive us. We don't have to wonder if what we did was too bad or if God might be angry with us. Jesus promised to forgive us, and He does.

# We Learn That God Loves Us, No Matter What

**Bible Verse**

"The LORD is . . . abounding in love. . . . He does not treat us as our sins deserve."

—Psalm 103:8, 10, NIV

Once there was a boy who had everything he needed, but he was still unhappy. *My father has lots of money,* he thought to himself. *Why should I just have one horse to ride? Maybe I want a whole herd of horses! Why should I just have the same number of games my brother has? Maybe I want more games!*

So he said to his father, "One day you will die, and half of what you own will be mine. Give me my half now, and I'll spend it on the things I want." This made his father very sad, but he did what his son asked. So the boy left his farm home happy and rich. He traveled to a big city and found a lot of new friends who helped him spend his money. They spent money on parties and toys and fancy food—and before long, the money was all spent. When the money was gone, the friends left too. The boy was all alone with nowhere to live and no food to eat.

When he was really hungry, he got a job feeding pigs. He didn't make much money, but he was so hungry that he ate the slop along with the pigs. He thought to himself, *This is gross. The people who work on my father's farm get to eat people food. I'll go home and ask if I can work there.*

So he traveled back to his father's house. When he got close, he saw someone running down the road toward him. It was his father! He said, "Father, I know I was stupid to take the money and spend it all. Just let me work here, and I won't bother you at all." But his father didn't even listen to him. He grabbed his boy up in a great big hug and said, "Oh, I'm so glad you're home! Come, let's have a party with all your favorite food. It's doesn't matter what happened before—you will always be my son and I will always love you."

God is like the father in this story. No matter what we do, no matter what we say, no matter where we go, we are His children. He loves us. And nothing— *nothing*—can ever change that.

And that's a mighty nice thing to know as we keep following Jesus.

## Teaching Tips

1. The parable of the prodigal son is a good story to dramatize and perform if you have a group of children who enjoy that sort of thing. And whenever they act out a story, they remember its lessons better.

2. Ask, "Why would someone who has everything be unhappy?" Possible answers might be no friends to play with, no one pays attention to him or her, etc. Point out that when you have everything, nothing is very important or special to you.

3. There is no way to overemphasize the unchangeable nature of God's love for us.

### Summary

No matter what we do, no matter what we say, no matter where we go, we are God's children. He loves us. And nothing—*nothing*— can ever change that.

# We Learn That It's What's Inside That Counts

## Bible Verse

" 'I will give you a new heart and put a new spirit in you.' "

—Ezekiel 36:26, NIV

Once I visited a family who grew apples. They had an orchard full of apple trees all lined up in long rows. Some of their trees grew red apples, some were a kind of golden color, and some were green. We walked out to where some of the trees were holding on to big, bright green apples that were just getting ripe.

"Pick one and taste it," my friends said. "These are the best apples you can eat."

So I searched all around one tree until I found an apple that looked perfect. Its bright green skin had no marks or bruises. It looked juicy and delicious! I grabbed it and pulled until it snapped off the branch. Then I polished it on my shirt and took the biggest bite I could!

As I started chewing, I held up the apple again. This time I saw something that made me stop chewing. There was a worm in my apple! Well, there was part of a worm in my apple. The rest of it was—I spit out the bite I had been chewing. Yuck!

I learned that you can't always tell a good apple by how it looks on the outside. It's the same way with being a Christian. Sometimes we think we can tell who are real Christians by looking at them. "That man is dressed nice. He's going to church. He must be a good Christian." Or, "Those kids are being nice to each other. No one is shouting or fighting. They must be good Christians." But we can't tell by looking. Some people dress nice and listen quietly to the pastor at church, but inside they are angry with everyone. And what about you? Have you ever pretended to be nice to your brothers or sisters because you want something from your mom?

It's what's inside our hearts that really counts. When we do the right things for the wrong reasons, we aren't being like Jesus at all. When we ask Jesus to change us so that we act like Him, He gives us a heart that's sweeter than any apple in the world. And that heart keeps us going on His path.

## Teaching Tips

1. Kids, especially boys, love gross things. Ask them to share the grossest thing they've ever eaten—like a worm in an apple. But watch out—they'll get carried away quickly!

2. Challenge the children to draw pictures of things that aren't always as good outside as they look inside. They will think of other foods, but suggest things like a book, a TV show or movie, a car, a house, or even a person.

3. Use the children to create a drama in which a kid acts nice to his or her siblings in order to get something from their mother, then is mean to them when she's not looking. Then do it again to show how a real Christian would act—nice whether anyone is watching or not.

### Summary

It's what's inside our hearts that really counts. When we ask Jesus to change us so that we act like Him, He gives us hearts that are sweeter than any apple in the world.

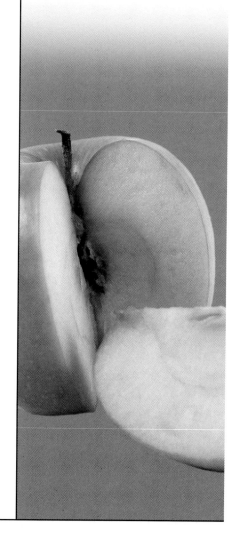

# We Learn About Being on Jesus' Team

**Bible Verse**

" 'All people will know that you are my followers if you love each other.' "

—John 13:35

Have you ever played football in the rain? I watched a football game that was played in the rain on television last week. It was hard for the players to keep the football in their hands when it was wet. It was hard for them to run without slipping in the mud. It was really hard to throw or kick the ball straight. I was glad not to be out there trying to play!

But it was a hard game for me to watch also. The players were falling and slipping and sliding in the mud, and before long, everyone was muddy. I couldn't tell which team was which! I wasn't sure when to cheer because I wasn't sure which players were on the team I liked. Since I couldn't see the color of their uniforms, I didn't know which players were on which team.

Can you tell a police officer when you see one? You can if he or she has a uniform and a badge on. Can you tell which person is a doctor or nurse in a hospital? Usually you can if you notice what they are wearing. These people, and many others, are dressed in ways that tell others who they are.

Sometimes we recognize people by the things they are doing. The person waving a baton in front of a band or choir is probably the conductor or leader. If you see a person up on a telephone or utility pole, he is probably someone who fixes telephone or electrical wires.

We can recognize Christians that way also. People see if we are following Jesus by the way we act and the things we say. They will see whether we eat or drink things that can destroy our bodies. They will see whether we are honest and trustworthy. But most important, they will see how we treat the people around us. Jesus told His disciples, " 'All people will know that you are my followers if you love each other' " (John 13:35).

We don't need a uniform to show people whether or not we are on Jesus' team. The way we treat each other will show people faster than any uniform or badge. It will be even clearer than waving a baton or climbing a pole. When we follow Jesus, we are kind to each other.

## Summary

We don't need a uniform to show people that we are on Jesus' team. The way we treat each other will show people we are Christians faster than any uniform or badge. When we follow Jesus, we are kind to each other.

## Teaching Tips

1. Help the children make a list of people we can identify by their uniforms or clothing. Ask, "Why is it important for people to be able to recognize them by how they look?" In discussing the value of knowing who's on our team or on our side in a war, or knowing who to turn to for help, ask, "Why is it important to be able to identify Christians by the way they act?"

2. Create a drama in which one child plays the part of a person who is wearing a police officer's uniform but isn't really one. When someone asks them for help, the person says No. Ask the children, "What will this person think about police officers now?" *(He or she will think that the police don't want to help or protect us.)* Then have a child play the part of a Christian (symbolized by carrying a Bible). When someone asks for help, the Christian says No. Ask the children, "What will this person think about Christians now?" *(He or she will think that the Christian doesn't really care about us or want to help other people.)*

# We Learn That We Can't Do It Ourselves

## Bible Verse

*"God is strong and can help you not to fall. He can bring you before his glory without any wrong in you and can give you great joy."*

—Jude 1:24, NCV

When I was growing up, my favorite place to play was in the backyard under the big sycamore tree. This tree had limbs that stretched far on each side, and it was much, much taller than the house. Being such a big tree, it had many big, strong limbs that went almost all the way to the top. I always wanted to climb up high in the tree and see how far I could see. There was only one problem. The first limb—the limb closest to the ground—was way over my head.

I tried to reach around the trunk and pull myself up, but I fell off. I tied a rope to my belt and threw the other end over the limb. Then I grabbed it and tried to pull myself up. My belt broke and my pants almost fell off. So that didn't work. What else could I try?

The ladder! It was strapped onto my dad's truck because he used it a lot. I raced to get it, but the truck was gone. I was stuck. I couldn't get up into the tree by myself.

When my dad got home, I showed him the limb. "Dad, I need the ladder to climb the tree."

Dad looked at the limb and then looked at me. "I don't know what we need a ladder for," he said. Then he stooped over and picked me up, lifting me higher than his head. I could reach the limb!

As I scrambled to sit there, he told me that I couldn't climb any higher until I got older. But I was in the tree, and I could see all the way across the field!

Being a Christian is like that too. No matter how hard we try, we can't make ourselves do the right thing all the time. We can't always remember to be kind. We aren't always honest. Just like I couldn't reach the limb and climb the tree, we can't be good all by ourselves. But Jesus is there to rescue us. If we ask Him to, He will pick us up and change us into people who remember more and more to act like He did. He will change our hearts.

We have to depend on Jesus to save us. And remembering that is the next important step in following Him.

## Teaching Tips

1. Ask, "What's the highest you've climbed by yourself? In a tree, on a ladder, in a tower or building?" Talk about how difficult or scary it was!

2. Help the children make a list of things they can't do by themselves, such as get to church, make a big dinner, clean out the gutters, shop for food, etc. Discuss who they need help from to get those things done.

3. Just for fun, bring in a big pair of boots. As each child tries the big boots on, challenge them to reach down and lift themselves up by the boots. Of course, they can't, so after they've had fun trying, talk about how we can't change our own hearts but we have to depend on Jesus to change us.

### Summary

No matter how hard we try, we can't be good all by ourselves. But Jesus is there to rescue us. If we ask Him to, He will pick us up and change us into people who act more and more like He did. He will change our hearts.

# We Learn to Keep Going and Keep Growing

As soon as our family got the new riding lawn mower, I wanted to mow the lawn more than anything else. I knew I could drive the lawn mower—it was just my size. "May I mow today? May I?" I asked my dad.

He just shook his head. "Nope. The yard doesn't need mowing today."

"Then may I just drive the lawn mower around?" I begged.

He shook his head again. "It's not a toy. Maybe you can mow on Friday."

I thought the week was never going to end. On Friday, I got home from school to see Dad driving the mower back and forth across the front yard. He stopped the mower and pulled me up onto the seat, saying, "If you want to mow, pay attention." I listened because I wanted to mow the lawn every week. "You have to drive in straight lines. Slow down when you reach the corners or you'll mow your mother's flowers." Finally it was my turn, and Dad went to sit on the porch and watch.

I kept the mower going straight until I had to duck to escape a bee. "Whoa!" I said when I saw that I was missing a whole strip of grass. I swerved to get back in line and missed cutting any grass at all. Then I forgot to slow down to turn and buzzed off a few flowers in the flower bed. I kept going, but before I got back to the porch, I knew it was a disaster.

Dad walked out as I turned off the mower. "I'm sorry," I mumbled. "I can't cut straight." I knew that he'd never let me mow again.

"It does look like a bad haircut," he agreed. Then he said, "Now this time around, go slower and try to keep your arms straight." I couldn't believe it! He wanted me to keep mowing!

It's easy to get discouraged when we mess up, even for a Christian. We sometimes get mad and say the wrong thing or get greedy and hold on to things that aren't ours. But when we're really sorry, Jesus forgives us and says, "Don't be discouraged. You're still learning. Keep going and keep growing." He doesn't give up on us. All we have to do is keep following His path.

## Teaching Tips

1. Share a personal story of making a mistake and being discouraged and then learning from it. It's good for children to realize that everyone makes mistakes, but take care because some children may get more ridicule than encouragement at home.

2. Help the children develop a list of the ways we mess up as Christians (tell a lie, get angry and hit someone, take something that isn't ours, etc.). Discuss what we should do then to make it right.

3. Play a game in which the children try to walk across the room balancing a book on their heads, or another game of your choice. Lead out in encouraging each one as the book falls.

### Summary

It's easy to get discouraged when we mess up. But when we're really sorry, Jesus forgives us and says, "Don't be discouraged. You're still learning. Keep going and keep growing." He doesn't give up on us.

# We Learn About Being Good—but Growing—Christians

**Bible Verse**

*"Grow in the grace and knowledge of our Lord and Savior Jesus Christ. Glory be to him now and forever! Amen."*

—2 Peter 3:18, NCV

Do you know what an acorn is? Acorns are the seeds of oak trees. They grow every summer at the ends of the branches with the leaves. In the fall, they drop to the ground. Squirrels love to eat them or hide them to eat later in winter. The only ones who love acorns as much as squirrels are kids—at least kids like me! I always thought that acorns were fun to play with. You can draw faces on them and glue them to sticks to make stick people. You can throw them or use them for slingshot ammo. Or you can collect them in a jar to leave out for squirrels who can't remember where their acorn treasures are hidden.

One of the trees near my house grew really big acorns—almost as big as quarters! I liked to take one of those acorns, pop its cap off, and carefully dig out the inside so that it was hollow. Then I'd put the cap back on, and it would be the perfect place to hide small treasures.

I learned something special about acorns: inside every acorn is a whole oak tree! No, you won't find a tiny tree if you cut one open. But if an acorn falls on the ground, and if a squirrel finds it before a kid picks it up, and if that squirrel doesn't eat it but digs a hole in the ground to hide it, and if it gets enough rain and sunshine, the acorn will start to grow. An acorn may not have limbs or leaves, but that doesn't make it a bad tree. It's just a tree that hasn't grown up yet.

Little roots will break through the acorn shell and grow down into the dirt. A little stem with tiny leaves will break through the dirt and stretch up into the sunshine. Every day it will grow bigger and bigger, more and more like a tree. And it all comes from that tiny acorn.

Young Christians are like acorns. Kids may not know as many Bible verses or understand as much as older Christians do, but that doesn't mean they're bad Christians. They're still growing and learning how to follow Jesus. Inside every one of us is a person who loves Jesus and wants to act just like Him. As long as we're following His path, we're growing a little more like Him every day.

## Teaching Tips

1. If possible, collect some acorns for the children (or with the children) to use along with craft sticks to make stick people. Talk about how an acorn has everything inside to be a big tree, just like children have everything inside them to be a grown-up and a Christian.

2. Ask, "What are the differences between you and your father or mother?" Point out that they are very close to the same *(ten fingers, ten toes, two eyes, etc.)* but not all grown up yet.

3. You may not be able to plant an acorn and have it sprout and grow, but try it with a bean. Let the children witness how it has everything inside to become a bean plant if it gets food and water.

### Summary

Young Christians are like acorns. They're still growing and learning how to follow Jesus. Inside every one of us is a person who loves Jesus and wants to act just like Him. As long as we're following His path, we're growing a little more like Him every day.

# We Learn We Must Stay Connected to Grow

### Bible Verse

*" 'No branch can produce fruit alone. It must remain in the vine. It is the same with you. You cannot produce fruit alone. You must remain in me.' "*

—John 15:4

Let's try an experiment. Go out into your yard and find a tree or bush that has a lot of small branches. Pick a spot where there are two very small branches close together (ask a parent to help you pick a good spot if you're not sure). Then snap or cut one of the branches off and take it with you. The next day, take your cut branch back out to the spot and compare it to the one still attached to the tree. Do they look the same?

Try it again in two days and in three days. Soon they will look very different. The one you snapped off will get dry and easy to break. The leaves will turn brown and fall off. But the one still attached to the tree will still be green and bendable.

Why are they different now? That's easy to answer. The one that is still connected to the tree is still alive and growing. It's still getting sunshine and water and tree food. The one that was snapped off is not connected, so it's not getting any of those things. It's dead.

Jesus did this same experiment with His friends. He showed them a grape vine and said, " 'No branch can produce fruit alone. It must remain in the vine. It is the same with you. You cannot produce fruit alone. You must remain in me' " (John 15:4).

Just like a branch will dry up and die if it's not connected to a tree, Christians dry up and die if they don't stay connected to Jesus. If they don't talk to Jesus by praying and learn about Jesus by reading or listening to stories about Him, then they stop growing. They stop following Jesus, so instead of becoming more like Him, they are less like Him every day.

We've been talking about following Jesus. Following Jesus is the same thing as staying connected to Him. If Jesus were talking to us today, He might say, "No one can grow up to be kind and honest and faithful if they follow a path going a different direction. You must follow My path if you want to be like Me. You must follow Me."

And that's exactly what we're learning to do!

## Teaching Tips

1. In a classroom, you can try this experiment with a potted plant. Break off a branch one week, and by the next week, the difference will be very easy to see.

2. Ask, "How does going to church help us stay connected to Jesus?" Discuss the value of getting together and praying, learning Bible stories, singing, etc.

3. Find some maze puzzles for children (the ones where you have to follow the right path through the lines without crossing any). Point out that it's the same when we follow Jesus—we can't get through the puzzle if we don't follow the right path.

### Summary

Just like a branch will dry up and die if it's not connected to a tree, Christians dry up and die if they don't stay connected to Jesus.

# We Learn About Changing Into Something New

**Bible Verse**

*"God has great mercy, and because of his mercy he gave us a new life."*

—1 Peter 1:3

Have you ever wished you could be a butterfly? You could float in the air, flying high with the wind and gliding slowly down to a flower. Well, it's not easy to become a butterfly—even for butterflies! A butterfly begins as an egg that hatches out as a small caterpillar that eats leaves. It eats and eats and grows and grows. Then when the time is right, it creates a special covering that hides it from the world—and the birds that would like to eat it! The caterpillar stays inside its special little house for a long time, and something wonderful happens. It grows and changes, and when it pops out, it's a beautiful butterfly! Its wings are stubby and wet at first, but the butterfly stretches them out and they dry. Soon the wings are strong, and the butterfly is ready to fly. It's one of the most amazing changes in nature.

Humans aren't like butterflies. Babies start off small, but they grow up to look like their parents. Still, there is one way that humans can change just as amazingly as caterpillars do.

Mr. Gilman owned a small store near our house when I was growing up. Whenever we were in his store, we might hear him shouting at his wife or kids. When he saw any kids come in the store, he would shout and tell them not to steal anything. We were afraid of him, and we didn't like going in his store at all. Even grown-ups grumbled about his trying to trick them into paying more than things cost and treating people rudely.

Then one summer, our church had meetings to tell people about Jesus. We sent notes to everyone in town inviting them to come. We were surprised when Mr. Gilman came with his family. At the end of the meetings, he decided to become a Christian and be baptized! From that day on, Mr. Gilman seemed like a different person. He was friendly when we came to his store. His wife and kids seemed much happier since he wasn't shouting at them anymore.

When Jesus changed Mr. Gilman's heart, it was just as amazing as seeing a caterpillar turn into a butterfly. Knowing that Jesus can change people—knowing that He is changing us—is the next big step along His path.

## Teaching Tips

1. Find a video or a set of photos to show the children the metamorphosis of a caterpillar into a butterfly. There is a good video at www.encarta.msn.com (search for "Monarch butterfly"). Talk about how God can change people too.

2. Invite the pastor or a church member to share their story of becoming a Christian and how God changed them.

## Summary

There is one way that we can change just as amazingly as caterpillars do when they change into butterflies. Jesus can change people's hearts from cross and mean to kind and friendly.

# We Learn What Jesus Was Like

" 'I tell you the truth, whoever believes in me will do the same things that I do.' "

—John 14:12, NCV

What did you do when you woke up this morning? Brushed your teeth, got dressed, ate your breakfast? After that you probably did different things depending on if it was a school day, Sabbath, or a holiday. Maybe you read a book or played a game or sang some songs.

Did you ever wonder what a day with Jesus would be like? Of course, Jesus lived a long time ago. When He traveled from one town to another, He didn't ride in a car or take a train. He walked. Jesus didn't seem to have a house of His own after He moved away from His mother. He stayed with friends or just slept outdoors.

If you spent a day with Jesus, what do you think you would see? Probably just what some friends of John the Baptist, Jesus' cousin, saw when they came to Jesus and asked, " 'Are you the man who John said was coming, or should we wait for another one?' " (Matthew 11:3). Jesus didn't answer them right away. Instead, He let them watch as He healed sick people and helped hurt people and told people about God. Then He said, " 'Go back to John and tell him about the things you hear and see: The blind can see. The crippled can walk. People with harmful skin diseases are healed. The deaf can hear. The dead are raised to life. And the Good News is told to the poor' " (Matthew 11:4, 5).

Jesus spent all His time helping people. He tried to make their lives better by healing them and by teaching them about God and His love. Over and over, He taught them, "God loves you, and He wants you to take care of each other."

The Bible doesn't tell us much about Jesus when He was a kid. But another wonderful book about Him, *The Desire of Ages,* says that while Jesus was growing up, He shared His food whenever someone was hungry. He cared about others, and He was so kind and thoughtful that everyone—old people, sad people, tired people, kids, even the little birds and animals, and the working donkeys and horses—everyone was happier when Jesus was around.

That's what Jesus did each day. He tried to make the people around Him happier and make the world a better place. And when we're following Jesus, we're doing that too.

## Summary

Jesus tried to make the people around Him happier and to make the world a better place. And when we're following Jesus, we'll do that too.

## Teaching Tips

1. Ask the children to make a list of the things they have done so far that day. Then ask, "How many of these things do you think Jesus did in His day?"

2. Help the children create a drama or write a story showing what a day spent with Jesus might have been like.

3. Ask, "What can we do today that will make the people at our church or home happier? What can we do to make our church or home a better place?" Then come up with a plan to do some of those things.

# We Learn to Exercise Our Kindness

**Bible Verse**

*"Be strong in the Lord and in his great power."*

—Ephesians 6:10, NCV

Have you ever broken your arm or leg? I did once when I was growing up. My brother and I liked to play football. Sometimes we tried to throw the ball farther than the other one could run to catch it. Sometimes we took turns trying to race past each other to score a touchdown. Usually, my brother could run faster, so it was hard for me to catch him. But when I had the ball, it was hard for him to knock or pull me down. One day when he pulled me down, I landed wrong on my arm. It looked OK on the outside, but it really hurt on the inside. My mom took me to the doctor, and he said my arm was broken. He put my arm in a cast to protect it and help it heal right.

So for a few weeks, I couldn't play football. Or ride my bike. Or do my homework! I couldn't use my arm to do anything. Finally, the day came when the doctor took off the cast and said my arm was all better. But it didn't look all better! It looked skinny and weak. And it was. Since I hadn't used my arm muscles in a long time, they had forgotten how to work. I could throw the football again, but I couldn't throw it very far. It took a few more weeks for my arm muscles to get strong again.

It works the same way for Christians. Because we're following Jesus, we're kind and helpful and honest. We're learning to be more like Jesus. And the same way muscles get stronger when we use them, we get better at being kind and helpful the more we do it. But if one day we choose to say something mean, if we decide to be selfish or decide to take something that doesn't belong to us, we start forgetting how to be a Christian. We start forgetting how to follow Jesus.

When we learn more about Jesus and try to act like He did, when we help others and tell them about God's love, we become stronger, better followers of Jesus. And that's what we want—we want to keep following Jesus.

## Summary

When we learn more about Jesus and try to act like He did, when we help others and tell them about God's love, we become stronger, better followers of Jesus.

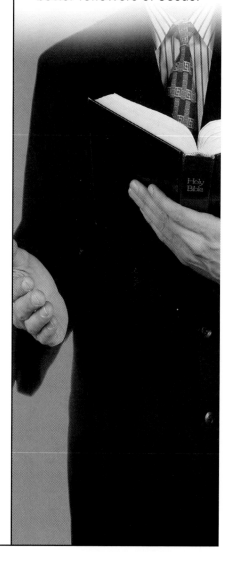

## Teaching Tips

1. Share a story of when you broke or injured an arm or leg, or ask a child to, and tell how it took time to grow strong again.

2. Have the children draw pictures to illustrate these ideas: If we want to grow stronger, we can work hard or lift weights. If we want to grow faster, we can eat healthful food and run a lot. Then, if we want to grow more like Jesus, what do we do?

3. If it's wise in your situation, consider bringing small hand weights to class. See which of the kids can lift the weights most easily or the most number of times. Of course, be very careful.

# We Learn to Work for God Wherever We Are

## Bible Verse

*"Do everything for the glory of God."*

—1 Corinthians 10:31

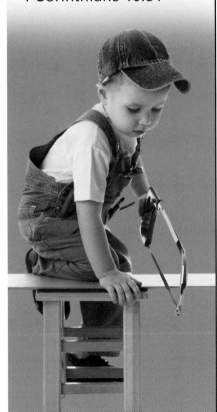

When we talk about being like Jesus, sometimes people think, I can't be like Jesus. I can't make sick people better or make blind people see. I can't preach to thousands of people or teach everyone about God. Even grown-ups feel that way. Most people aren't preachers or teachers. Doctors and nurses work hard to help sick people get well, but no one today can fix people like Jesus did. So can we really be like Him?

Let's think about the years that Jesus lived. When He was your age, He was going to school, and His mother was His teacher. When He was old enough, He went to work in Joseph's carpenter shop. He probably worked cutting boards and building chairs and making ladders with Joseph for at least fifteen years. Then He left home and started teaching people about God every day. But Jesus only spent three years teaching and healing people before He died. So most of His life, He worked all day just like everyone else. And every day that He worked sawing boards and hammering nails, He was doing what God wanted Him to do.

Jesus worked hard and did His best in the carpenter shop. He was always kind and helpful when He was in school. He looked for ways to help people understand God's love when He was preaching and teaching. He was always doing what God wanted Him to do and acting the way God wanted Him to act.

It's the same with us. It doesn't matter whether we're in school or on the playground or at home with our family—we can always be like Jesus. We can always be kind and helpful and honest. We can't take away people's colds or make their broken arms all better. But we can offer to help them with chores or homework. We can't help it if sometimes people are sad or lonely or have problems. But we can be friendly and polite and look for ways to cheer them up or help them.

The Bible says, "Whether you eat or drink or whatever you do, do it all for the glory of God" (1 Corinthians 10:31, NIV). If we remember that when we're in school or playing a game or working at home, then we'll be acting just like Jesus did. And we'll be following the path He left for us.

## Teaching Tips

1. Ask each child, "What do you want to be when you grow up?" Discuss how they will be working for God no matter what they do.

2. With the help of the children, make a list of the things we can't do for people; but balance it with a list of things we can do. For example, we can't heal sick people, bring back lost or dead pets, make it all better when someone is sad, keep someone's parents from getting divorced, etc. But we can help sick people by doing their chores, or help sad people by comforting them or looking for ways to cheer them up.

3. This would be an ideal occasion to do a craft in which the children build or create something. As they work, remind them that Jesus was doing God's work while He was building things in the carpenter shop.

## Summary

It doesn't matter whether we're in school or on the playground or at home with our families—we can always be like Jesus. We can always be kind and helpful and honest.

# We Learn From God's Two Books

## Bible Verse

*"The Bereans were eager to hear what Paul and Silas said and studied the Scriptures every day to find out if these things were true."*

—Acts 17:11, NCV

People who come to visit at my house can learn two things about me just by looking around. I have a whole room full of bookshelves and nearly all of those shelves are filled with books. And the spaces without books are filled with animals—stuffed toy animals, animals carved from wood, and animals made of plastic. So anyone who visits can see right away that I like books and I like animals!

What would we learn about you if we looked in your room? Would we see what kind of sports you like to play or what kinds of animals you like? Would we learn if you like to read or like to play games?

We can learn things about God by looking around at what He created. When we see butterflies floating in our backyard, or stars twinkling in the sky at night, or a rainbow after a rainstorm, we learn that God loves beautiful things. When we see the sun rise and set each day, and the moon and stars appear when they should each night, we learn that God has a plan for everything. And when we hear a bullfrog croak or taste tangerines or watch a monkey swing in a tree, we learn that God likes fun things!

We can also learn about God from the Bible. The stories in the Bible tell us what happens when people listen to God and follow Him—and what happens when they don't. The Bible tells us that God loves people who are beautiful on the inside—people who are kind and honest. It is full of stories about people who are learning to follow God, learning to listen to Him, and learning to live the way He wants them to.

We learn the most about God from the Bible's stories about Jesus. The way Jesus treated people—the way He healed the sick and comforted the ones who were lonely or sad—tells us how much God loves every person. It also tells us how God wants us to treat people around us every day at home, at school, or on the playground.

The more we learn about God, the easier it is to follow Jesus.

## Teaching Tips

1. Ask, "What would we learn about you from your room? Or what would we learn about your family from your house?"

2. Have the children write or tell one of their favorite stories from the Bible. Help them think through what that story tells us about God.

3. Help the children create a play in which they try to answer the question "What is God like?" by showing Christians in action.

### Summary

We can learn things about God by looking at what He created. But we learn the most about God from the Bible's stories about Jesus. The way Jesus treated people tells us how much God loves every person. It also tells us how God wants us to treat people around us every day at home, at school, or on the playground.

# We Learn to Talk to God as a Friend

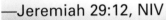

" 'Then you will call upon me and come and pray to me, and I will listen to you.' "

—Jeremiah 29:12, NIV

One day I came home from school with homework. I had to find an important person and ask him or her some questions. I asked my mom, "Who is the most important person in our town?" She said, "I guess the mayor is the most important person. He's like the boss of our town." So I decided that I would ask the mayor my questions.

It wasn't easy to get to talk to the mayor. He was very busy. My mom helped me call his office several times, trying to plan a meeting with him. Finally, his assistant said, "You can come to the mayor's office tomorrow afternoon. But you'll only have five minutes to ask your questions."

I wrote down my questions and practiced asking them to my friend Kevin. But still, when we went to the mayor's office, my hands were kind of shaky and I felt like caterpillars were running races in my stomach. It was much harder to ask him the questions than it was to ask Kevin. He was nice, but I was so glad when I was finished!

Some people think prayer is like talking to a very important person. They get nervous and try to use big words. Sometimes they write their prayers down or try to memorize them. But even though God is a very important Person, we don't have to be nervous about talking to Him. Praying to God is like talking to a friend.

That doesn't mean that we joke or tease with God like we might with our friends. It means that we can just talk about the things we think about or the things that are bothering us. It means we can tell God how we feel when we're afraid of bees or bad guys. It means we can tell Him that we're sad about a lost puppy or sad when someone we love dies. And we can tell Him how much we liked His rainbow that day or how funny we think ostriches look.

Knowing that we can talk to God like a friend is a big step in learning to follow Jesus.

## Teaching Tips

1. Ask, "Who is the most important person you know? What questions would you ask him or her if you could?"

2. Ask the pastor or an older church member to talk to the children about prayer. Suggest that they emphasize praying all during the day instead of just at night or at mealtimes.

3. To practice this kind of praying, have the students write a letter to God. Encourage them to write it the way they would write to a friend.

### Summary

Even though God is a very important Person, we don't have to be nervous about talking to Him. Praying to God is like talking to a friend.

# We Learn Why We Go to Church

### Bible Verse

*"You should not stay away from the church meetings, as some are doing, but you should meet together and encourage each other."*

—Hebrews 10:25, NCV

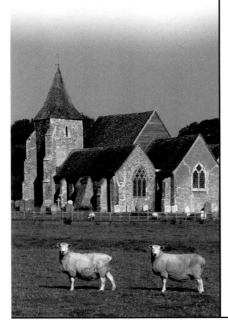

Have you even seen a flock of sheep in a field? If you have, you've seen that all the sheep stay close together. The flock may move slowly across the field as they graze—eat grass—but they all move together. When it's time for a drink, the whole flock goes to the stream or water hole. Sheep are herd animals; that is, they don't like to be alone. They like to have other sheep around them.

Being together all the time is a good thing for sheep. If a sheep was grazing in a field all alone, it would be in danger every time it put its head down to the grass. With its head down, it couldn't see any danger that might be coming. When the flock is eating grass in a field, some have their heads up while others are eating. Some are always watching out for danger. When it's cold, they all huddle together to stay warm.

The Bible says that people are like sheep. Christians follow Jesus like sheep follow a shepherd—the person who takes care of them. Jesus liked to say, "I am the Good Shepherd." He said, " 'My sheep listen to my voice. I know them, and they follow me' " (John 10:27).

One of the ways that Christians are like sheep is that being together is a good thing for them. Being together to worship is important for Christians. When

Christians meet together, they feel safer because they can help each other stay away from dangerous things. They feel stronger because they can study the Bible together and talk about God's love. They feel closer to God because they feel God's love when they take care of each other and pray for each other.

Christians are also a lot like a family—a big family in which everyone watches out for each other. Just like a regular family, a church family works together to keep the kids safe and teach them about God's love. They work together to have a nice church building. And they work together to tell others about Jesus.

We go to church because it makes us stronger, better Christians. Together, a church family can follow Jesus like sheep follow a shepherd.

## Teaching Tips

1. Ask, "What other animals live in large groups like sheep do? Why do you think Jesus said He was like a shepherd and His people like sheep?" *(Sheep were common where Jesus lived, unlike cows, horses, elk, zebras, antelope, or other herd animals.)*

2. Have the children make a list of the things they like about church. Be sure to explore why they like each item. Point out examples of the blessings of being part of a church family.

3. Send the children out to interview church members or family members. They could ask, "What do you like most about church? Does the church seem like a family to you? Why?"

### Summary

Christians are really a lot like a family—a big family in which everyone watches out for each other. Just like a regular family, a church family works together to keep the kids safe and teach them about God's love.

# We Learn That We'll Always Have Questions

### Bible Verse

*"Now we see a dim reflection, as if we were looking into a mirror, but then we shall see clearly."*

—1 Corinthians 13:12, NCV

There is a big mirror on one of the doors in my house. It helps me see what I look like—from my shirt collar all the way down to my shoes—before I go out. When my grandson Ethan was just old enough to crawl, he came to my house for a visit. I was standing in front of the mirror one morning when Ethan crawled to my feet and sat down. He saw the baby in the mirror and laughed. The baby laughed too. Ethan clapped his hands, and the baby clapped too!

Before long, Ethan crawled over to the mirror and put out his hand to touch the baby. All he felt was the smooth mirror. He tried again. This time the mirror moved because the door wasn't shut and he was pushing it. That gave him an idea. He crawled over to the edge of the door and looked around behind it, expecting to find the baby back there. But it wasn't there!

Ethan crawled back to my mirror every day he was at my house to look for that baby. He wasn't old enough to understand that the baby he saw was him! He didn't understand that a mirror just reflects whatever is in front of it.

There are a lot of things we don't understand when we're young. We don't understand why zebras have stripes but horses don't. We don't understand why green leaves turn yellow and red and brown in the fall. And we don't understand why people have to die.

There are many things we don't understand when we're all grown up either. We might not understand why our car stops working or why there are so many mosquitoes at our picnic. And we still don't always understand why people have to get sick or get in accidents and die.

There are many things we can learn from the Bible about God and His plans for us. But the Bible doesn't answer all our questions. There will always be more to learn and more questions to ask. Just because we don't have all the answers doesn't mean that God isn't there or that He doesn't care. It means that we're not ready or able to understand yet. But God promises that someday in heaven we can ask all our questions and learn the answers.

Knowing that we'll always have questions is a very important step in learning to follow Jesus.

### Summary

There are many things we can learn from the Bible about God and His plans for us. But the Bible doesn't answer all our questions. There will always be more to learn and more questions to ask.

## Teaching Tips

1. If possible, tell the children a story about something you believed when you were young or that a child you know believed. Encourage them to share things they thought were true when they were younger

2. Help the children make a list of the things they don't know such as, "I don't know what the sun does at night," or "I don't know why my cat died," or "I don't know how so much rain gets up in the sky," etc. Encourage them to be creative and imaginative by suggesting a few questions yourself!

3. Invite the pastor or a church leader to meet with the children to answer some of their questions if possible. Encourage him or her to point out that we will always have questions and that it's OK for Christians to question things.

# We Learn to Be a Witness

### Bible Verse

" 'When the Holy Spirit comes to you, you will receive power. You will be my witnesses . . . in every part of the world.' "

—Acts 1:8, NCV

Yesterday I saw a strange thing in the sky. It was up high and a long way away, but it looked like a long flying box! It got closer and closer until I could see that it was flat, like a superbig, really long sheet of paper. And there was a picture on it and some words. When it was close enough, I heard the sound of an airplane, and finally I figured out what it was. A small airplane was pulling a really big sign right through the air! The sign was a picture of an elephant saying, "Come see me at the zoo!"

It was an advertisement—a way to tell people about the zoo. You see advertisements every day on television, in magazines, on big billboards by the road, and on the sides of buses and trucks. Companies use advertisements to talk to us and say, "Come learn about us" or "Buy the things that we sell."

We also send messages to tell others about ourselves. We send letters to our grandparents or e-mails to our friends to share the things we're doing. If we're away from home, we call our parents on the phone to tell them that we're OK and that we miss them.

We've learned that God sends us messages about Himself too. We learn about Him from the things we see in nature and from the stories we read in the Bible. But how does God talk to people who don't read the Bible? How does He send messages to people who have never heard about Jesus and His love?

God has a very special way of sending a message to people like that—He sends you and me! Every Christian carries a message about God with him or her every day. Everything we say and do tells the people around us something about God. That's what being a witness means—sharing what we know about God's love with others.

We can witness by telling others what we know about God or telling them how to find out more about God in the Bible. But we can also witness by treating people with kindness the way Jesus did. Any time we help someone, we are sending a message that says, "I care about you because God cares about me. And He cares about you too."

Learning that we are witnesses every day is another big step in following Jesus.

## Teaching Tips

1. Clip some ads out of newspapers or magazines. Show them to the children and help them figure out what the ad is telling them. You will have to choose ads carefully. Try to help the children see what the pictures are saying *(You'll be happy if you buy this, only smart people shop here, etc.)* as well as what the words of the ad are saying.

2. Ask, "What are you telling others about God when you're happy? What are you telling them about God when you're mean? What are you telling others about God when you're kind?"

3. Have the children decorate cards that say, "I care about you because God cares about me. And He cares about you too!" Then hand them out to people at church or to family members at home.

## Summary

Every Christian carries a message about God with him or her every day. Everything we say and do tells the people around us something about God.

# We Learn to Look for the Good

**Bible Verse**

*"I will be happy because of you; / God Most High, I will sing praises to your name."*

—Psalm 9:2, NCV

Emma and Samantha went on a hike through the woods. They stuck together, following the same trail, and they got home at the same time. "How was your hike?" their mom asked.

Emma was bouncing up and down. "It was wonderful! We saw two squirrels chasing each other, and a bright red bird flew right past my head. Look, I picked one of the beautiful blue flowers we saw and brought it home for you!"

Samantha slumped into a chair. "It was awful," she moaned. "Every plant I touched had thorns. It was hot and the ground was muddy. A bee buzzed right past my head and almost stung me! And look, there's a scratch on my arm where a tree limb scraped me."

Both girls went on the same hike, but Samantha could only think about the things she didn't like, so she had a bad time. Emma walked past the same thorns and was in the same mud, but she remembered the good things. So she had a fun hike.

Being a Christian doesn't mean that bad things won't happen to you. God treats all people the same. Jesus said, " 'He causes the sun to rise on good people and on evil people, and he sends rain to those who do right and to those who do wrong' " (Matthew 5:45, NCV). But being like Jesus means looking for the good things in life.

Maybe you aren't the best baseball player, but you can still have fun playing with your friends. Maybe there is one kid in your class who bothers you, but you can be happy that other kids are your friends. Maybe you don't have as many toys or games as some of your friends, but you can still be happy with the ones you have.

You can decide if you're going to look for and remember the good things each day—things that make you laugh, fun with friends and family, or the bad things—mean people, mistakes you make, things you don't get to do.

Learning to look for the good things will make you more like Jesus. It will make you a happy person who everyone enjoys being with.

## Teaching Tips

1. Ask, "Why do you think God doesn't have good things happen just to good people and let bad things happen to bad people?"

2. Help the children make a list of the good things that have happened to them recently and a list of the bad things. Encourage them to focus on the good things.

3. Go for a walk with the children. Point out the things that make everyone smile or laugh. No doubt some negative things will happen, but at the end, point out how much fun it was to find the good things.

### Summary

Being a Christian doesn't mean that bad things won't happen to you. But being like Jesus means looking for the good things in life.

# We Learn to Trust God's Plan

## Bible Verse

*"Jesus answered, 'I am the way, and the truth, and the life.'"*

—John 14:6, NCV

Have you ever woken up suddenly at night when it's dark and you aren't sure where you are? I remember waking up once in the middle of the night because my bed bounced. Well, it wasn't really my bed. I was in my family's car, and we were going to visit my grandparents. I looked out the window, but it was too dark to see anything. I was worried. "Where are we?" I asked my dad, who was driving.

"We're halfway between where we were and where we're going to be in the morning. Now go back to sleep." That didn't tell me anything, but I felt better because Dad was driving and he wasn't worried. Then I fell asleep. When I woke up, we were driving up to a place to eat breakfast. That worried me. "I don't know if I like the food here," I said. My dad laughed. "Don't worry. We'll find something you like."

When we started driving again, I watched out the windows. There weren't any trees or hills like the ones near my house. *What if we get lost?* I worried. "Dad, are you sure you know how to get to Grandma's house?" I asked.

He smiled. "Don't worry. I've driven on this road many times. I know the way."

Before long, I found out that he was right. I was silly to worry because we drove right up to my grandma's house!

Being a Christian is like being on a long journey. Even though we are following Jesus, there may be many times when we aren't sure what to think. Things may happen that make us worried or sad. It might be easy to say, "I don't know why this is happening. Why isn't God helping me?" That's when you have to trust God's plan and believe that He knows what is best.

Jesus said, "You don't need to worry. You can believe in God and in Me. My Father's house has many rooms, and I'm going to fix one just for you. Then I'm coming back to take you home with Me forever" (John 14:1–3, author adaptation).

Following Jesus is a great adventure. There will always be questions to ask and things to learn. But every step will make you a happier person and a better person. And Jesus will be with you all along the way.

## Summary

Following Jesus is a great adventure. There will always be questions to ask and things to learn. But every step will make us happier and better people. And Jesus will be with us all along the way.

## Teaching Tips

1. Share a story about a time when you got lost or almost got lost. How did you find the way? A map? Asked someone who knew?

2. Ask, "What kinds of things make you worried or sad? Whom do you talk to when you're worried or sad?"

3. Ask each child to draw a map from their house to church or school or some other prominent place. They may need to work with a parent or adult who knows the way, someone they trust. Point out how we must trust God when we don't know the way.

# Quotations From *Steps to Christ*

The steps outlined in this book are based on principles gleaned from *Steps to Christ,* Ellen White's wonderful guide to Christian living. The selections below correspond to each of this book's steps.

## Step 1. We learn that God loves us

" 'God is love' is written upon every opening bud, upon every spire of springing grass. The lovely birds making the air vocal with their happy songs, the delicately tinted flowers in their perfection perfuming the air, the lofty trees of the forest with their rich foliage of living green—all testify to the tender, fatherly care of our God and to His desire to make His children happy.

"The word of God reveals His character. He Himself has declared His infinite love and pity. When Moses prayed, 'Show me Thy glory,' the Lord answered, 'I will make all My goodness pass before thee.' Exodus 33:18, 19. This is His glory. The Lord passed before Moses, and proclaimed, 'The Lord, The Lord God, merciful and gracious, long-suffering, and abundant in goodness and truth, keeping mercy for thousands, forgiving iniquity and transgression and sin.' Exodus 34:6, 7. He is 'slow to anger, and of great kindness,' 'because He delighteth in mercy.' Jonah 4:2; Micah 7:18.

"God has bound our hearts to Him by unnumbered tokens in heaven and in earth. Through the things of nature, and the deepest and tenderest earthly ties that human hearts can know, He has sought to reveal Himself to us. Yet these but imperfectly represent His love" (p. 10).

## Step 2. We learn what God is like

"The Son of God came from heaven to make manifest the Father. 'No man hath seen God at any time; the only begotten Son, which is in the bosom of the Father, He hath declared Him.' John 1:18. 'Neither knoweth any man the Father, save the Son, and he to whomsoever the Son will reveal Him.' Matthew 11:27. When one of the disciples made the request, 'Show us the Father,' Jesus answered, 'Have I been so long time with you, and yet hast thou not known Me, Philip? He that hath seen Me hath seen the Father; and how sayest thou then, Show us the Father?' John 14:8, 9.

"In describing His earthly mission, Jesus said, The Lord 'hath anointed Me to preach the gospel to the poor; He hath sent Me to heal the brokenhearted, to preach deliverance to the captives, and recovering of sight to the blind, to set at liberty them that are bruised.' Luke 4:18. This was His work. He went about doing good and healing all that were oppressed by Satan. There were whole villages where there was not a moan of sickness in any house, for He had passed through them and healed all their sick. His work gave evidence of His divine anointing. Love, mercy, and compassion were revealed in every act of His life; His heart went out in tender sympathy to the children of men. He took man's nature, that He might reach man's wants. The poorest and humblest were not afraid to approach Him. Even little children were attracted to Him. They loved to climb upon His knees and gaze into the pensive face, benignant with love" (pp. 11, 12).

## Step 3. We learn why God loves us

" 'God so loved the world, that He gave His only-begotten Son.' He gave Him not only to live among men, to bear their sins, and die their sacrifice. He gave Him to the fallen race. Christ was to identify Himself with the interests and needs of humanity. He who was one with God has linked Himself with the children of men by ties that are never to be broken. Jesus is 'not ashamed to call them brethren' (Hebrews 2:11); He is our Sacrifice, our Advocate, our Brother, bearing our human form before the Father's throne, and through eternal ages one with the race He has redeemed—the Son of man. And all this that man might be uplifted from the ruin and degradation of sin that he might reflect the love of God and share the joy of holiness" (p. 14).

## Step 4. We learn what we can't do

"It is impossible for us, of ourselves, to escape from the pit of sin in which we are sunken. Our hearts are evil, and we cannot change them.

'Who can bring a clean thing out of an unclean? not one.' ' The carnal mind is enmity against God: for it is not subject to the law of God, neither indeed can be.' Job 14:4; Romans 8:7. Education, culture, the exercise of the will, human effort, all have their proper sphere, but here they are powerless. They may produce an outward correctness of behavior, but they cannot change the heart; they cannot purify the springs of life. There must be a power working from within, a new life from above, before men can be changed from sin to holiness. That power is Christ. His grace alone can quicken the lifeless faculties of the soul, and attract it to God, to holiness" (p. 18)

## Step 5. We learn that Jesus connects us to heaven

"It is not enough to perceive the loving-kindness of God, to see the benevolence, the fatherly tenderness, of His character. It is not enough to discern the wisdom and justice of His law, to see that it is founded upon the eternal principle of love. Paul the apostle saw all this when he exclaimed, 'I consent unto the law that it is good.' ' The law is holy, and the commandment holy, and just, and good.' But he added, in the bitterness of his soul-anguish and despair, 'I am carnal, sold under sin.' Romans 7:16, 12, 14. He longed for the purity, the righteousness, to which in himself he was powerless to attain, and cried out, 'O wretched man that I am! who shall deliver me from this body of death?' Romans 7:24, margin. Such is the cry that has gone up from burdened hearts in all lands and in all ages. To all, there is but one answer, 'Behold the Lamb of God, which taketh away the sin of the world.' John 1:29.

"Many are the figures by which the Spirit of God has sought to illustrate this truth, and make it plain to souls that long to be freed from the burden of guilt. When, after his sin in deceiving Esau, Jacob fled from his father's home, he was weighed down with a sense of guilt. Lonely and outcast as he was, separated from all that had made life dear, the one thought that above all others pressed upon his soul, was the fear that his sin had cut him off from God, that he was forsaken of Heaven. In sadness he lay down to rest on the bare earth, around him only the lonely hills, and above, the heavens bright with stars. As he slept, a strange light broke upon his vision; and lo, from the plain on which he lay, vast shadowy stairs seemed to lead upward to the very gates of heaven, and upon them angels of God were passing up and down; while from the glory above, the divine voice was heard in a message of comfort and hope.

Thus was made known to Jacob that which met the need and longing of his soul—a Saviour. With joy and gratitude he saw revealed a way by which he, a sinner, could be restored to communion with God. The mystic ladder of his dream represented Jesus, the only medium of communication between God and man" (pp. 19, 20).

## Step 6. We learn about being sorry when we do wrong things

"Repentance includes sorrow for sin and a turning away from it. We shall not renounce sin unless we see its sinfulness; until we turn away from it in heart, there will be no real change in the life.

"There are many who fail to understand the true nature of repentance. Multitudes sorrow that they have sinned and even make an outward reformation because they fear that their wrongdoing will bring suffering upon themselves. But this is not repentance in the Bible sense. They lament the suffering rather than the sin. Such was the grief of Esau when he saw that the birthright was lost to him forever. Balaam, terrified by the angel standing in his pathway with drawn sword, acknowledged his guilt lest he should lose his life; but there was no genuine repentance for sin, no conversion of purpose, no abhorrence of evil. Judas Iscariot, after betraying his Lord, exclaimed, 'I have sinned in that I have betrayed the innocent blood.' Matthew 27:4" (pp. 23, 24).

"True confession is always of a specific character, and acknowledges particular sins. They may be of such a nature as to be brought before God only; they may be wrongs that should be confessed to individuals who have suffered injury through them; or they may be of a public character, and should then be as publicly confessed. But all confession should be definite and to the point, acknowledging the very sins of which you are guilty" (p. 38).

## Step 7. We learn that really being sorry means changing

"Confession will not be acceptable to God without sincere repentance and reformation. There must be decided changes in the life; everything offensive to God must be put away. This will be the result of genuine sorrow for sin. The work that we have to do on our part is plainly set before us: 'Wash you, make you clean; put away the evil of your doings from before Mine eyes; cease to do evil; learn to do well; seek judgment, relieve the oppressed, judge the fatherless, plead for the widow.' Isaiah 1:16, 17. 'If the wicked restore the pledge, give again that he had robbed, walk in the statutes of life, without committing iniquity; he shall surely live, he shall not die.' Ezekiel 33:15. Paul says, speaking of the work of repentance: 'Ye sorrowed after a godly sort, what carefulness it wrought in you, yea, what clearing of yourselves, yea, what indignation, yea, what fear, yea, what vehement desire, yea, what zeal, yea, what revenge! In all things ye have approved yourselves to be clear in this matter.' 2 Corinthians 7:11" (p. 39).

## Step 8. We learn to apologize to other people

"True repentance will lead a man to bear his guilt himself and acknowledge it without deception or hypocrisy. Like the poor publican, not lifting up so much as his eyes unto heaven, he will cry, 'God be merciful to me a sinner,' and those who do acknowledge their guilt will be justified, for Jesus will plead His blood in behalf of the repentant soul.

"The examples in God's word of genuine repentance and humiliation reveal a spirit of confession in which there is no excuse for sin or attempt at self-justification. Paul did not seek to shield himself; he paints his sin in its darkest hue, not attempting to lessen his guilt. He says, 'Many of the saints did I shut up in prison, having received authority from the chief priests; and when they were put to death, I gave my voice against them. And I punished them oft in every synagogue, and compelled them to blaspheme; and being exceedingly mad against them, I persecuted them even unto strange cities.' Acts 26:10, 11. He does not hesitate to declare that 'Christ Jesus came into the world to save sinners; of whom I am chief.' 1 Timothy 1:15" (pp. 40, 41).

## Step 9. We learn that God wants us to be happy

"God does not require us to give up anything that it is for our best interest to retain. In all that He does, He has the well-being of His children in view. Would that all who have not chosen Christ might realize that He has something vastly better to offer them than they are seeking for themselves. Man is doing the greatest injury and injustice to his own soul when he thinks and acts contrary to the will of God. No real joy can be found in the path forbidden by Him who knows what is best and who plans for the good of His creatures. The path of transgression is the path of misery and destruction" (p. 46).

## Step 10. We learn about choosing to believe

"Many are inquiring, 'How am I to make the surrender of myself to God?' You desire to give yourself to Him, but you are weak in moral power, in slavery to doubt, and controlled by the habits of your life of sin. Your promises and resolutions are like ropes of sand. You cannot control your thoughts, your impulses, your affections. The knowledge of your broken promises and forfeited pledges weakens your confidence in your own sincerity, and causes you to feel that God cannot accept you; but you need not despair. What you need to understand is the true force of the will. This is the governing power in the nature of man, the power of decision, or of choice. Everything depends on the right action of the will. The power of choice God has given to men; it is theirs to exercise. You cannot change your heart, you cannot of yourself give to God its affections; but you can choose to serve Him. You can give Him your will; He will then work in you to will and to do according to His good pleasure. Thus your whole nature will be brought under the control of the Spirit of Christ; your affections will be centered upon Him, your thoughts will be in harmony with Him.

"Desires for goodness and holiness are right as far as they go; but if you stop here, they will avail nothing. Many will be lost while hoping and desiring to be Christians. They do not come to the point of yielding the will to God. They do not now choose to be Christians" (pp. 47, 48).

## Step 11. We learn that God wants us to have peace

"As your conscience has been quickened by the Holy Spirit, you have seen something of the evil of sin, of its power, its guilt, its woe; and you look upon it with abhorrence. You feel that sin has separated you from God, that you are in bondage to the power of evil. The more you struggle to escape, the more you realize your helplessness. Your motives are impure; your heart is unclean. You see that your life has been filled with selfishness and sin. You long to be forgiven, to be cleansed, to be set free. Harmony with God, likeness to Him—what can you do to obtain it?

"It is peace that you need—Heaven's forgiveness and peace and love in the soul. Money cannot buy it, intellect cannot procure it, wisdom cannot attain to it; you can never hope, by your own efforts, to secure it. But God offers it to you as a gift, 'without money and without price.' Isaiah 55:1. It is yours if you will but reach out your hand and grasp it. The Lord says, 'Though your sins be as scarlet, they shall be as white as snow; though they be red like crimson, they shall be as wool.' Isaiah 1:18. 'A new heart also will I give you, and a new spirit will I put within you.' Ezekiel 36:26" (p. 49).

## Step 12. We learn we can believe Jesus' promises

"From the simple Bible account of how Jesus healed the sick, we may learn something about how to believe in Him for the forgiveness of sins. Let us turn to the story of the paralytic at Bethesda. The poor sufferer was helpless; he had not used his limbs for thirty-eight years. Yet Jesus bade him, 'Rise, take up thy bed, and walk.' The sick man might have said, 'Lord, if Thou wilt make me whole, I will obey Thy word.' But, no, he believed Christ's word, believed that he was made whole, and he made the effort at once; he *willed* to walk, and he did walk. He acted on the word of Christ, and God gave the power. He was made whole.

"In like manner you are a sinner. You cannot atone for your past sins; you cannot change your heart and make yourself holy. But God promises to do all this for you through Christ. You *believe* that promise. You confess your sins and give yourself to God. You *will* to serve Him. Just as surely as you do this, God will fulfill His word to you. If you believe the promise—believe that you are forgiven and cleansed—God supplies the fact; you are made whole, just as Christ gave the paralytic power to walk when the man believed that he was healed. It is so if you believe it.

"Do not wait to feel that you are made whole, but say, 'I believe it; it is so, not because I feel it, but because God has promised' " (pp. 50, 51).

## Step 13. We learn that God loves us, no matter what

"God does not deal with us as finite men deal with one another. His thoughts are thoughts of mercy, love, and tenderest compassion. He says, 'Let the wicked forsake his way, and the unrighteous man his thoughts: and let him return unto the Lord, and He will have mercy upon him; and to our God, for He will abundantly pardon.' 'I have blotted out, as a thick cloud, thy transgressions, and, as a cloud, thy sins.' Isaiah 55:7; 44:22.

" 'I have no pleasure in the death of him that dieth, saith the Lord God: wherefore turn yourselves, and live ye.' Ezekiel 18:32. Satan is ready to steal away the blessed assurances of God. He desires to take every glimmer of hope and every ray of light from the soul; but you must not permit him to do this. Do not give ear to the tempter, but say, 'Jesus has died that I might live. He loves me, and wills not that I should perish. I have a compassionate heavenly Father; and although I have abused His love, though the blessings He has given me have been squandered, I will arise, and go to my Father, and say, "I have sinned against heaven, and before Thee, and am no more worthy to be called Thy son: make me as one of Thy hired servants." ' The parable tells you how the wanderer will be received: 'When he was yet a great way off,' his father saw him, and had compassion, and ran, and fell on his neck, and kissed him.' Luke 15:18–20.

"But even this parable, tender and touching as it is, comes short of expressing the infinite compassion of the heavenly Father" (pp. 53, 54).

## Step 14. We learn that it's what's inside that counts

"It is true that there may be an outward correctness of deportment without the renewing power of Christ. The love of influence and the desire for the esteem of others may produce a well-ordered life. Self-respect may lead us to avoid the appearance of evil. A selfish heart may perform generous actions. By what means, then, shall we determine whose side we are on?

"Who has the heart? With whom are our thoughts? Of whom do we love to converse? Who has our warmest affections and our best energies? If we are Christ's, our thoughts are with Him, and our sweetest thoughts are of

Him. All we have and are is consecrated to Him. We long to bear His image, breathe His spirit, do His will, and please Him in all things" (p. 58).

## Step 15. We learn about being on Jesus' team

"If our hearts are renewed in the likeness of God, if the divine love is implanted in the soul, will not the law of God be carried out in the life? When the principle of love is implanted in the heart, when man is renewed after the image of Him that created him, the new-covenant promise is fulfilled, 'I will put My laws into their hearts, and in their minds will I write them.' Hebrews 10:16. And if the law is written in the heart, will it not shape the life? Obedience—the service and allegiance of love—is the true sign of discipleship. Thus the Scripture says, 'This is the love of God, that we keep His commandments.' 'He that saith, I know Him, and keepeth not His commandments, is a liar, and the truth is not in him.' 1 John 5:3; 2:4. Instead of releasing man from obedience, it is faith, and faith only, that makes us partakers of the grace of Christ, which enables us to render obedience" (pp. 60, 61).

## Step 16. We learn that we can't do it ourselves

"So Jesus said to His disciples, 'It is not ye that speak, but the Spirit of your Father which speaketh in you.' Matthew 10:20. Then with Christ working in you, you will manifest the same spirit and do the same good works—works of righteousness, obedience.

"So we have nothing in ourselves of which to boast. We have no ground for self-exaltation. Our only ground of hope is in the righteousness of Christ imputed to us, and in that wrought by His Spirit working in and through us" (p. 63).

## Step 17. We learn to keep going and keep growing

"The closer you come to Jesus, the more faulty you will appear in your own eyes; for your vision will be clearer, and your imperfections will be seen in broad and distinct contrast to His perfect nature. This is evidence that Satan's delusions have lost their power; that the vivifying influence of the Spirit of God is arousing you.

"No deep-seated love for Jesus can dwell in the heart that does not realize its own sinfulness. The soul that is transformed by the grace of

Christ will admire His divine character; but if we do not see our own moral deformity, it is unmistakable evidence that we have not had a view of the beauty and excellence of Christ.

"The less we see to esteem in ourselves, the more we shall see to esteem in the infinite purity and loveliness of our Saviour. A view of our sinfulness drives us to Him who can pardon; and when the soul, realizing its helplessness, reaches out after Christ, He will reveal Himself in power. The more our sense of need drives us to Him and to the word of God, the more exalted views we shall have of His character, and the more fully we shall reflect His image" (pp. 64, 65).

## Step 18. We learn about being good—but growing— Christians

"The change of heart by which we become children of God is in the Bible spoken of as birth. Again, it is compared to the germination of the good seed sown by the husbandman. In like manner those who are just converted to Christ are, 'as new-born babes,' to 'grow up' to the stature of men and women in Christ Jesus. 1 Peter 2:2; Ephesians 4:15. Or like the good seed sown in the field, they are to grow up and bring forth fruit. Isaiah says that they shall 'be called trees of righteousness, the planting of the Lord, that He might be glorified.' Isaiah 61:3. So from natural life, illustrations are drawn, to help us better to understand the mysterious truths of spiritual life" (p. 67).

## Step 19. We learn we must stay connected to grow

"Jesus teaches the same thing when He says, 'Abide in Me, and I in you. As the branch cannot bear fruit of itself, except it abide in the vine; no more can ye, except ye abide in Me. . . . Without Me ye can do nothing.' John 15:4, 5. You are just as dependent upon Christ, in order to live a holy life, as is the branch upon the parent stock for growth and fruitfulness. Apart from Him you have no life. You have no power to resist temptation or to grow in grace and holiness. Abiding in Him, you may flourish. Drawing your life from Him, you will not wither nor be fruitless. You will be like a tree planted by the rivers of water.

"Many have an idea that they must do some part of the work alone. They have trusted in Christ for the forgiveness of sin, but now they seek by their own efforts to live aright. But every such effort must fail. Jesus says,

'Without Me ye can do nothing.' Our growth in grace, our joy, our usefulness—all depend upon our union with Christ. It is by communion with Him, daily, hourly—by abiding in Him—that we are to grow in grace" (pp. 68, 69).

## Step 20. We learn about changing into something new

"Even John, the beloved disciple, the one who most fully reflected the likeness of the Saviour, did not naturally possess that loveliness of character. He was not only self-assertive and ambitious for honor, but impetuous, and resentful under injuries. But as the character of the Divine One was manifested to him, he saw his own deficiency and was humbled by the knowledge. The strength and patience, the power and tenderness, the majesty and meekness, that he beheld in the daily life of the Son of God, filled his soul with admiration and love. Day by day his heart was drawn out toward Christ, until he lost sight of self in love for his Master. His resentful, ambitious temper was yielded to the molding power of Christ. The regenerating influence of the Holy Spirit renewed his heart. The power of the love of Christ wrought a transformation of character. This is the sure result of union with Jesus. When Christ abides in the heart, the whole nature is transformed. Christ's Spirit, His love, softens the heart, subdues the soul, and raises the thoughts and desires toward God and heaven" (p. 73).

## Step 21. We learn what Jesus was like

"Love to Jesus will be manifested in a desire to work as He worked for the blessing and uplifting of humanity. It will lead to love, tenderness, and sympathy toward all the creatures of our heavenly Father's care.

"The Saviour's life on earth was not a life of ease and devotion to Himself, but He toiled with persistent, earnest, untiring effort for the salvation of lost mankind. From the manger to Calvary He followed the path of self-denial and sought not to be released from arduous tasks, painful travels and exhausting care and labor. He said, 'The Son of man came not to be ministered unto, but to minister, and to give His life a ransom for many.' Matthew 20:28. This was the one great object of His life. Everything else was secondary and subservient. It was His meat and drink to do the will of God and to finish His work. Self and self-interest had no part in His labor" (pp. 77, 78).

## Step 22. We learn to exercise our kindness

"The only way to grow in grace is to be disinterestedly doing the very work which Christ has enjoined upon us—to engage, to the extent of our ability, in helping and blessing those who need the help we can give them. Strength comes by exercise; activity is the very condition of life. Those who endeavor to maintain Christian life by passively accepting the blessings that come through the means of grace, and doing nothing for Christ, are simply trying to live by eating without working. And in the spiritual as in the natural world, this always results in degeneration and decay. A man who would refuse to exercise his limbs would soon lose all power to use them. Thus the Christian who will not exercise his God-given powers not only fails to grow up into Christ, but he loses the strength that he already had" (pp. 80, 81).

## Step 23. We learn to work for God wherever we are

"The greater part of our Saviour's life on earth was spent in patient toil in the carpenter's shop at Nazareth. Ministering angels attended the Lord of life as He walked side by side with peasants and laborers, unrecognized and unhonored. He was as faithfully fulfilling His mission while working at His humble trade as when He healed the sick or walked upon the storm-tossed waves of Galilee. So in the humblest duties and lowliest positions of life, we may walk and work with Jesus.

"The apostle says, 'Let every man, wherein he is called, therein abide with God.' 1 Corinthians 7:24. The businessman may conduct his business in a way that will glorify his Master because of his fidelity. If he is a true follower of Christ he will carry his religion into everything that is done and reveal to men the spirit of Christ. The mechanic may be a diligent and faithful representative of Him who toiled in the lowly walks of life among the hills of Galilee. Everyone who names the name of Christ should so work that others, by seeing his good works, may be led to glorify their Creator and Redeemer" (pp. 81, 82).

## Step 24. We learn from God's two books

"Many are the ways in which God is seeking to make Himself known to us and bring us into communion with Him. Nature speaks to our senses without ceasing. The open heart will be impressed with the love and glory of God as revealed through the works of His hands. The listening ear can hear and understand the communications of God through the things of nature. The green fields, the lofty trees, the buds and flowers, the passing cloud, the falling rain, the babbling brook, the glories of the heavens, speak to our hearts, and invite us to become acquainted with Him who made them all.

"Our Saviour bound up His precious lessons with the things of nature. The trees, the birds, the flowers of the valleys, the hills, the lakes, and the beautiful heavens, as well as the incidents and surroundings of daily life, were all linked with the words of truth, that His lessons might thus be often recalled to mind, even amid the busy cares of man's life of toil.

"God would have His children appreciate His works and delight in the simple, quiet beauty with which He has adorned our earthly home. He is a lover of the beautiful, and above all that is outwardly attractive He loves beauty of character; He would have us cultivate purity and simplicity, the quiet graces of the flowers. If we will but listen, God's created works will teach us precious lessons of obedience and trust" (p. 85).

"God speaks to us in His word. Here we have in clearer lines the revelation of His character, of His dealings with men, and the great work of redemption. Here is open before us the history of patriarchs and prophets and other holy men of old. They were men 'subject to like passions as we are.' James 5:17. We see how they struggled through discouragements like our own, how they fell under temptation as we have done, and yet took heart again and conquered through the grace of God; and, beholding, we are encouraged in our striving after righteousness. As we read of the precious experiences granted them, of the light and love and blessing it was theirs to enjoy, and of the work they wrought through the grace given them, the spirit that inspired them kindles a flame of holy emulation in our hearts and a desire to be like them in character—like them to walk with God.

"Jesus said of the Old Testament Scriptures—and how much more is it true of the New—'They are they which testify of Me,' the Redeemer, Him in whom our hopes of eternal life are centered. John 5:39. Yes, the whole Bible tells of Christ. From the first record of creation—for 'without Him was not anything made that was made'—to the closing promise, 'Behold, I come quickly,' we are reading of His works and listening to His voice. John 1:3; Revelation 22:12. If you would become acquainted with the Saviour, study the Holy Scriptures" (pp. 87, 88).

## Step 25. We learn to talk to God as a friend

"Prayer is the opening of the heart to God as to a friend. Not that it is necessary in order to make known to God what we are, but in order to enable us to receive Him. Prayer does not bring God down to us, but brings us up to Him" (p. 93).

## Step 26. We learn why we go to church

"We sustain a loss when we neglect the privilege of associating together to strengthen and encourage one another in the service of God. The truths of His word lose their vividness and importance in our minds. Our hearts cease to be enlightened and aroused by their sanctifying influence, and we decline in spirituality. In our association as Christians we lose much by lack of sympathy with one another. He who shuts himself up to himself is not filling the position that God designed he should. The proper cultivation of the social elements in our nature brings us into sympathy with others and is a means of development and strength to us in the service of God.

"If Christians would associate together, speaking to each other of the love of God and of the precious truths of redemption, their own hearts would be refreshed and they would refresh one another. We may be daily learning more of our heavenly Father, gaining a fresh experience of His grace; then we shall desire to speak of His love; and as we do this, our own hearts will be warmed and encouraged. If we thought and talked more of Jesus, and less of self, we should have far more of His presence" (pp. 101, 102).

## Step 27. We learn that we'll always have questions

"The word of God, like the character of its divine Author, presents mysteries that can never be fully comprehended by finite beings. The entrance of sin into the world, the incarnation of Christ, regeneration, the resurrection, and many other subjects presented in the Bible, are mysteries too deep for the human mind to explain, or even fully to comprehend. But we have no reason to doubt God's word because we cannot understand the mysteries of His providence. In the natural world we are constantly surrounded with mysteries that we cannot fathom. The very humblest forms of life present a problem that the wisest of philosophers is powerless to explain. Everywhere are wonders beyond our ken. Should we then be surprised to find that in the spiritual world also there are mysteries that we cannot fathom? The difficulty lies solely in the weakness and narrowness of the human mind. God has given us in the Scriptures sufficient evidence of their divine character, and we are not to doubt His word because we cannot understand all the mysteries of His providence.

"The apostle Peter says that there are in Scripture 'things hard to be understood, which they that are unlearned and unstable wrest . . . unto their own destruction.' 2 Peter 3:16. The difficulties of Scripture have been urged by skeptics as an argument against the Bible; but so far from this, they constitute a strong evidence of its divine inspiration. If it contained no account of God but that which we could easily comprehend; if His greatness and majesty could be grasped by finite minds, then the Bible would not bear the unmistakable credentials of divine authority. The very grandeur and mystery of the themes presented should inspire faith in it as the word of God" (pp. 106, 107).

## Step 28. We learn to be a witness

"The children of God are called to be representatives of Christ, showing forth the goodness and mercy of the Lord. As Jesus has revealed to us the true character of the Father, so we are to reveal Christ to a world that does not know His tender, pitying love. 'As Thou hast sent Me into the world,' said Jesus, 'even so have I also sent them into the world.' 'I in them, and Thou in Me; . . . that the world may know that Thou hast sent Me.' John 17: 18, 23. The apostle Paul says to the disciples of Jesus, 'Ye are manifestly declared to be the epistle of Christ,' 'known and read of all men.' 2 Corinthians 3:3, 2. In every one of His children, Jesus sends a letter to the world. If you are Christ's follower, He sends in you a letter to the family, the village, the street, where you live. Jesus, dwelling in you, desires to speak to the hearts of those who are not acquainted with Him. Perhaps they do not read the Bible, or do not hear the voice that speaks to them in its pages; they do not see the love of God through His works. But if you are a true representative of Jesus, it may be that through you they will be led to understand something of His goodness and be won to love and serve Him.

"Christians are set as light bearers on the way to heaven. They are to reflect to the world the light shining upon them from Christ. Their life and character should be such that through them others will get a right conception of Christ and of His service" (p. 115).

## Step 29. We learn to look for the good

"Have there not been some bright spots in your experience? Have you not had some precious seasons when your heart throbbed with joy in response to the Spirit of God? When you look back into the chapters of your life experience do you not find some pleasant pages? Are not God's promises, like the fragrant flowers, growing beside your path on every hand? Will you not let their beauty and sweetness fill your heart with joy?

"The briers and thorns will only wound and grieve you; and if you gather only these things, and present them to others, are you not, besides slighting the goodness of God yourself, preventing those around you from walking in the path of life?

"It is not wise to gather together all the unpleasant recollections of a past life—its iniquities and disappointments—to talk over them and mourn over them until we are overwhelmed with discouragement. A discouraged soul is filled with darkness, shutting out the light of God from his own soul and casting a shadow upon the pathway of others.

"Thank God for the bright pictures which He has presented to us. Let us group together the blessed assurances of His love, that we may look upon them continually: The Son of God leaving His Father's throne, clothing His divinity with humanity, that He might rescue man from the power of Satan; His triumph in our behalf, opening heaven to men, revealing to human vision the presence chamber where the Deity unveils His glory; the fallen race uplifted from the pit of ruin into which sin had plunged it, and brought again into connection with the infinite God, and having endured the divine test through faith in our Redeemer, clothed in the righteousness of Christ, and exalted to His throne—these are the pictures which God would have us contemplate" (pp. 117, 118).

## Step 30. We learn to trust God's plan

"It is not the will of God that His people should be weighed down with care. But our Lord does not deceive us. He does not say to us,

'Do not fear; there are no dangers in your path.' He knows there are trials and dangers, and He deals with us plainly. He does not propose to take His people out of a world of sin and evil, but He points them to a never-failing refuge. His prayer for His disciples was, 'I pray not that Thou shouldest take them out of the world, but that Thou shouldest keep them from the evil.' 'In the world,' He says, 'ye shall have tribulation: but be of good cheer; I have overcome the world.' John 17:15, 16:33.

"In His Sermon on the Mount, Christ taught His disciples precious lessons in regard to the necessity of trusting in God. These lessons were designed to encourage the children of God through all ages, and they have come down to our time full of instruction and comfort. The Saviour pointed His followers to the birds of the air as they warbled their carols of praise, unencumbered with thoughts of care, for 'they sow not, neither do they reap.' And yet the great Father provides for their needs. The Saviour asks, 'Are ye not much better than they?' Matthew 6:26. The great Provider for man and beast opens His hand and supplies all His creatures. The birds of the air are not beneath His notice. He does not drop the food into their bills, but He makes provision for their needs. They must gather the grains He has scattered for them. They must prepare the material for their little nests. They must feed their young. They go forth singing to their labor, for 'your heavenly Father feedeth them.' And 'are ye not much better than they?' Are not you, as intelligent, spiritual worshipers, of more value than the birds of the air? Will not the Author of our being, the Preserver of our life, the One who formed us in His own divine image, provide for our necessities if we but trust in Him?

"Christ pointed His disciples to the flowers of the field, growing in rich profusion and glowing in the simple beauty which the heavenly Father had given them, as an expression of His love to man. He said, 'Consider the lilies of the field, how they grow.' The beauty and simplicity of these natural flowers far outrival the splendor of Solomon. The most gorgeous attire produced by the skill of art cannot bear comparison with the natural grace and radiant beauty of the flowers of God's creation. Jesus asks, 'If God so clothe the grass of the field, which today is, and tomorrow is cast into the oven, shall He not much more clothe you, O ye of little faith?' Matthew 6: 28, 30. If God, the divine Artist, gives to the simple flowers that perish in a day their delicate and varied colors, how much greater care will He have for those who are created in His own image? This lesson of Christ's is a rebuke to the anxious thought, the perplexity and doubt, of the faithless heart.

"The Lord would have all His sons and daughters happy, peaceful, and obedient. Jesus says, 'My peace I give unto you: not as the world giveth, give I unto you. Let not your heart be troubled, neither let it be afraid.' 'These things have I spoken unto you, that My joy might remain in you, and that your joy might be full.' John 14:27; 15:11" (pp. 122–124).